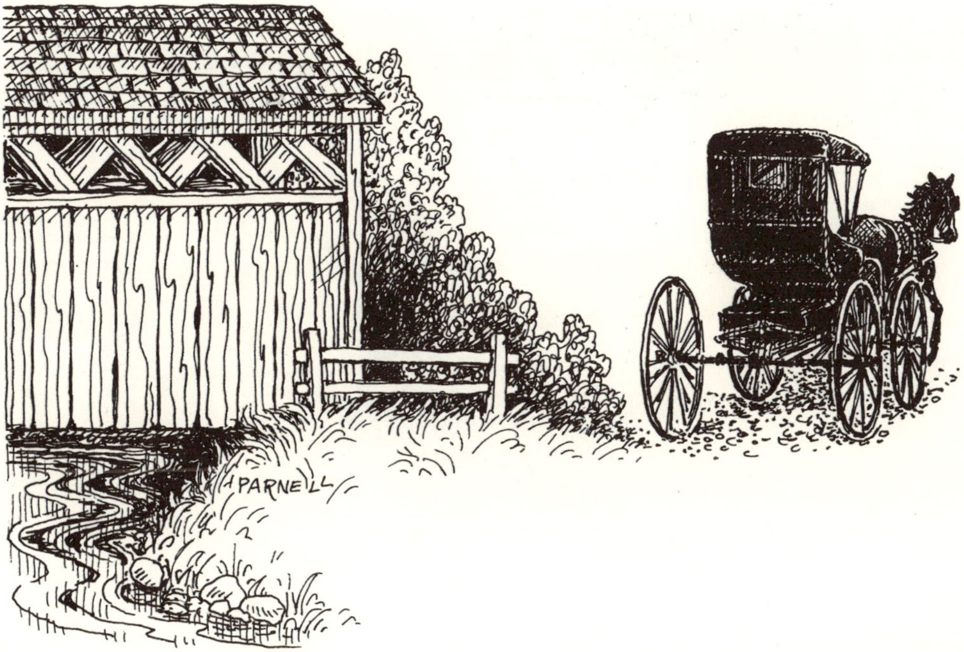
PARNELL

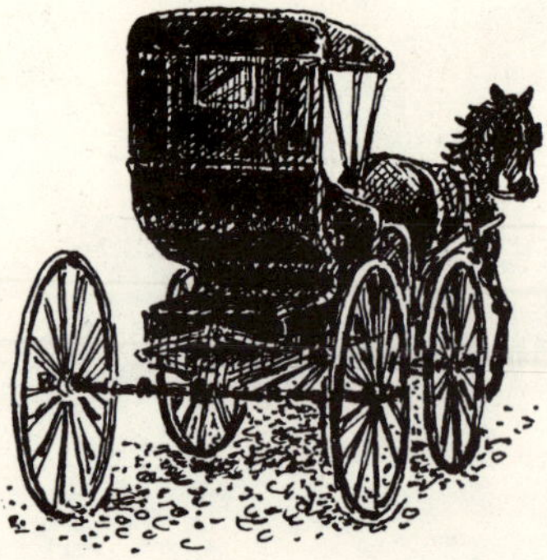

The Country Doctor Alive and Well

A commonsense approach to your whole health.

THE COUNTRY DOCTOR

ALIVE AND WELL

A Story of Love for the Land and its People

by

John G. Hipps, M.D.
In collaboration with Barbiann Smith

A commonsense approach to your whole health.

Published by

GOOD EARTH PUBLISHING

RR 1 North Creek

Emporium, PA 15934

www.thecountrydoctor.com
cntrydoc@penn.com

Copyright © 1999 by John G. Hipps, M.D. All rights reserved.

Permission to reproduce or transmit in any form or by any means, electronic or mechanical, including photocopying and recording, or by any information storage and retrieval system must be obtained by writing to the publisher.

Publishers Cataloging-in-Publication

Hipps, John G
    The country doctor, alive and well: a story of love for the land and its people / by John G. Hipps in collaboration with Barbiann Smith.--1st ed.
    p. cm.
    ISBN: 0-9623758-0-2

    1. Hipps, John G. 2. Medicine, Rural. 3. Physicians--Biography. 4. Self-care, Health. I. Title

R154.H57A3 1999   610'.92 [B]
                      QBI99-998

Published by
Good Earth Publishing
RR 1 North Creek
Emporium, PA 15834

Publication Date - January 2000

Acknowledgments

One of the privileges of authorship, beyond the pleasure of the book's dedication, is the opportunity to acknowledge certain individuals who have been essential to its accomplishment:

Margie Slover Willis of Willis Transcription Service in Westfield, Pennsylvania, whose creative services were vital to this book's journey from my mind and heart to the handwritten and the dictated word. Without her computer talents, the task would have been infinitely more difficult and time-consuming.

Susan Parnell, *Highlights for Children* artist of Roulette, Pennsylvania, who designed the front and back covers and the interior black and white graphics.

Mary Catherine McLean and Laural Lynne Coppock of Emporium, Pennsylvania, whose multiple talents and dedication to innumerable details helped immeasurably to power the book's successful journey from paper to the hands of the readers.

Editor Barbara Weber Lewis, from Houston, Texas, who gave the manuscript a professional touch.

Graphic designer H. Tooter Randall of A & S Enterprises, Inc., Coudersport, Pennsylvania for making the cover and inside graphics camera ready.

The "patient" and the tens of thousands of people who have fit that special description in my life of the past forty years, whether or not their presence has honored my own medical office or that of another. Without you, my professional and personal life would be far less worthwhile.

Disclaimers

Susquehoning is a fictitious name intended to ensure anonymity for actual places and to preserve personal confidentiality. Although not a mythical place, it is often mystical, frequently magical, and always real. Its character, its people, and its happenings commonly denominate an assortment of locales throughout the Appalachian Mountain Range and the world. Any similarity with real places and people is unintended and coincidental. It is virtual and not actual reality.

Story and Interlude content is intended to inform and entertain. It is not meant to advise or treat. The reader's personal health provider should be consulted, in a timely manner, for proper diagnosis and treatment.

Oft it has been said, "There is nothing new under the sun in word or deed, in story or song; there are but new twists to old truths." Such is the truth applicable to the authorship of the quotes and quips which begin and end each chapter. No claim of personal ownership is asserted by this author. Instead, credit is acknowledged to whomever it is due, be it the first grunts of our earliest ancestors, the eloquent tongues of great minds of all ages since, specific individuals, or the anonymous.

Dedicated to Barbiann,

*my friend and companion,
my sweetheart and wife.*

Her physical, mental, and spiritual contributions to this endeavor, and to my life, have been so immense, so multi-dimensional, that I am without words to express them.

Her presence on the back cover, viewing the panoramic scene out of which these stories emerge, symbolizes the strength of her own creativity and emphasizes the power of her penetrating insights into every page, every line, every word.

Contents

Author's Note
Prelude
From Country Doctors to HMO's

Chapter Titles   Interlude
Titles

Chapter 1   Bell-Bottom Trousers   1
     Interlude 1   Anxiety   12
Chapter 2   Cake Walk   13
     Interlude 2   Some Quick Fixes   21
Chapter 3   Fetal Physician   22
     Interlude 3   Insomnia   30
Chapter 4   Big George   31
     Interlude 4   Whatisitis?   41
Chapter 5   Say Ahhh   43
     Interlude 5   More Quick Fixes   49
Chapter 6   On the Run   50
     Interlude 6   Common Sense and
                        Fitness   61
Chapter 7   Sugar and Spice   62
     Interlude 7   Symptoms and Signs   72

Chapter 8	Old Scrooge	73
Interlude 8	Headache	81
Chapter 9	What! A Helicopter	82
Interlude 9	Phobia	87
Chapter 10	Curbstone Experts	88
Interlude 10	Still More Quick Fixes	98
Chapter 11	Black Foot Country	99
Interlude 11	Acutupps	106
Chapter 12	Hills of Home	107
Interlude 12	A Final Fix	113
Chapter 13	Miracle Child	114
Interlude 13	A Blessed Trinity	118
Chapter 14	Harmon's Little Acre	119
Interlude 14	Memory	126
Chapter 15	Sweet and Low	127
Interlude 15	How Low is Hypo?	132
Chapter 16	Jack Spratt and Millie	134
Interlude 16	Target Organs	142
Chapter 17	In To Africa	144
Interlude 17	Potpourri	158
Chapter 18	Jenny's Zoo	159
Interlude 18	Vitamins or Not	168
Chapter 19	Hill Farming	170
Interlude 19	Fatigue	176
Chapter 20	Snow Birds	177
Interlude 20	Morepourri	184

Chapter 21	Tincture of Time	185
Interlude 21	Depression	191
Chapter 22	Down on the Farm	193
Interlude 22	Stillmorpourri	203
Chapter 23	Vet For a Day	204
Interlude 23	Acceptance	212
Chapter 24	A Brain Game	214
Interlude 24	This is a Medical IQ Test	220
Chapter 25	Copter Doctor	222
Interlude 25	Life is a Risk	233
Chapter 26	Different Strokes for Different Folks	234
Interlude 26	A Patch for a Pill	242
Chapter 27	Home Baked Bread	244
Interlude 27	Common Sense and Nutrition	250
Chapter 28	Rip's Van Wrinkle	252
Interlude 28	To Sleep or Not to Sleep	257
Chapter 29	Myai	258
Interlude 29	Some Finalpourri	265
Chapter 30	Rambling Wrecks	266
Interlude 30	Bumps and Bruises	270
Chapter 31	Miss Lottie	271
Interlude 31	Wrinkles	281

Chapter 32 A Pint's a Pound   283
    Interlude 32   Common Sense and
                    Weight   290
Chapter 33 Tell Me a Story   292
    Interlude 33   I Can Believe That   298
Chapter 34 David and Goliath   299
    Interlude 34   Cabin Fever   308
Chapter 35 Flatlanders and
            Ridgerunners   309
    Interlude 35   I Can Believe
                    That Too   316
Chapter 36 The Healing Woods   317
    Interlude 36   Trigger Points   325
Chapter 37 Live and Let Die   326
    Interlude 37   Common Sense and
                    Stress   331
Chapter 38 Happy Town   332
    Interlude 38   Common Sense and
                    Wellness   342
Chapter 39 There's No Place
            Like Home   344
    Interlude 39   Patient Wisdom   353
Chapter 40 A Long, Long
            Trail A-Winding   355

About the Author   364

Author's Note

As our world stands on tiptoe at the threshold of tumultuous change, does a place remain for the simple and the compassionate, for love and lightness of heart?

It is my belief that today's doctors--no matter their specialty, no matter where and what they practice, no matter how they are managed--can nurture the caring, compassionate spirit that, in elder days, endeared the country doctor to the hearts of his patients. It can be so despite the cancerous growth and the brutal business of managed care, where non-medical players operate under the influence of power and money. The wish, the want, the need continues along with the hope that the spirit will prevail and bind us together in everyday encounters with patients, families, and friends.

This collection of memories is meant to personify that spirit, confirming its undaunted presence and encouraging its perpetuation in the heart of humankind. There has been no intent at autobiography. The sequence of stories has no rhyme nor reason other than to share what I hope will enlighten and amuse. I have simply penned a potpourri of spontaneously triggered memorable experiences with patients and people, as each cherished day comes and goes.

John G. Hipps, M.D.

Prelude

It was daybreak in Appalachian Mountain Country. Tips of the surrounding hills slowly emerged out of a misty sea of fog that filled the valleys. Dawn's waking light echoed with the clop of a horse on the plank floor of the covered bridge that spanned Anderson Creek.

Through the mist and out of the nineteenth century, a horse and buggy appeared. A country doctor held the lines with a confidence matched by that of his horse whose head was held high in staunch determination. Both were ready to face the adventures of a new day.

A few years down the road, that same horse was reined to a stop as the doctor greeted me.

"Good morning, son. Are you ready to go with us this bright and beautiful day?"

"You betcha, sir!" I replied, excited at the prospect of making country house calls again.

"Take the reins," he prompted. "I want to check my bag before we make our first call at the next farm."

I felt like a royal coachman as I guided our horse down the road with an occasional shift of the reins. The mystery of the black bag beneath the seat could wait for another time, when the doctor was ready to reveal its secrets to me.

Now this is real horse power, I thought. There is no need for a choke or a throttle here, just a "giddy-up" or a "whoa". A click of the tongue against my teeth, along with a quiet word or two now and then, accomplished the rest. The whip that sat in the holder on the knee board just in front of me would never be used on the animal. But, it was a great way to keep the pesky flies away.

At the turn of the century, telephones were few and far between. Each village had one at the doctor's office and one at the post office. Calls for help came by word of mouth, on foot, or the doctor's intuitive sense that someone was in need. Usually, he was right.

Those were the glory days of youth when I was honored to share in the life of an old-time country doctor. He has remained a constant inspiration every day throughout the years.

My dear old friend closed out the nineteenth century and opened up the twentieth with his special brand of compassion and caring, pure and simple. It would be a special privilege to one day do the same with my end of the twentieth century and my journey into the twenty-first.

From Country Doctors to HMOs

In way bygone days, anyone needing medical attention went to the country doctor. As life in the United States became less rural, it was the family doctor. Life moved on and the general practitioner was the one to see. Now, we have the primary care physician who may be an internist, obstetrician, gynecologist, or pediatrician.

Specialists moved steadily into the scene over the past 25 years and many people took on the family surgeon and pediatrician, the family neurologist and dermatologist, the family chiropractor and psychologist, and so on and so on and so forth.

The family lawyer quickly appeared and is now often the first professional to be consulted for matters of illness and injury.

The picture continues to change. We now speak of our family emergency room and the family HMO.

Now, that's quite a switch from the nineteenth-century country doctor and the early twentieth-century general practitioner.

And that gives you an idea of what's become of simplicity and common sense in today's complex and sometimes nonsense health care scene.

Chapter 1

Bell-Bottom Trousers

Uncertainty gives life added zest.

The USS *Colbert*, A.P.A. 145, was slowly sinking into a very deep ocean. We had struck a mine on our port side exactly amidship, where the engine room was located. A hole as large as a two-story house gaped open letting the wild South Pacific sea pour in. A huge air bubble belched out as water gushed in to fill the entire compartment. All power was gone. We were a sitting duck in a very big bathtub.

And, I couldn't do a thing about it. Nor could my 399 shipmates.

It had all happened so quickly. There was only one ominous thud, as though the ship had run aground against the tip of a submerged lava island. I had been literally knocked out of my bunk and into the cramped corridor. Too stunned to realize what had happened, I focused my energy on keeping my balance while the ship lurched from side to side, taking water across the deck with each roll. It was the first time in rough water that I did not become seasick. The thought never entered my mind.

I staggered through the corridor in the direction of the sick bay, then realized I was without my life jacket. It hung on my bunk at night and on my back at all other times. One of my shipmates had snatched it. Frightened and desperate, I settled for a life belt, much less effective, and rushed to my battle station to care for the wounded.

It was my assignment, as a Navy hospital corpsman, to combat enemy attack by keeping as many men behind as many guns for as many minutes as possible. Although that was a very military mind set, contrary to the Hippocratic Oath I was to live by for a lifetime, it was one I could appreciate as Japanese kamikaze fighter planes were shot out of the sky before they had a chance to crash into my ship.

I continued to function, although I was considerably unnerved that the ship was sinking. Death, you know, may be common, even anticipated in a war zone, but it's a more special event when it's your own.

It is well known that when a person faces impending death, a life full of happenings flash across the movie screen of the mind. My first near-death experience took place in one of my childhood swimming holes. At the age of six years, with a height of three feet, I had stepped into a four-foot drop off. It wasn't until I was going down for

Alive and Well

the third time, after a lot of sputtering and gurgling, that my companions had come to my rescue.

But this situation was different. I was no longer three feet tall. I was five feet four inches, and the Yellow Sea was a thousand feet deep. A 150-mile per hour typhoon whipped the water into 40-foot waves.

The ship continued to settle downward until I could reach over the side and touch the water. Then, it stopped. The inner bulkheads of the engine room held fast and kept the ocean out of the other compartments. We stayed afloat, just barely. I shudder to think how quickly we would have bottomed out to the briny deep had that mine penetrated the adjacent compartment.

The typhoon threatened to swamp even the biggest of warships. Only the day before, I had stood on deck, watching battleships and heavy cruisers tossed like corks, end to end, and taking on water with each massive rock.

Our own troop transport of the Liberty Ship Class was much lighter, more boxy. It was taking on water over both ends and both sides, threatening to turn keel up at any moment. In light of our predicament, it was not a comforting thought to remember its nickname, Kaiser's Coffin.

The *Colbert* was one in an entire fleet of warships returning from Korea with our own prisoners of war. Ships were bobbing around like apples in a Halloween

The Country Doctor

tub. The *Colbert* bobbed less, due to the weight of the water that filled our engine compartment.

The storm raged for two days. As the wildness of the waters subsided, our emergency call for help was answered by a nearby heavy cruiser, the USS *Tuscaloosa*. Our two ships jockeyed as close as possible for three hours while our rescue ship attempted to jettison a towline to us. After several near misses, the *Colbert* finally snagged our end of their line, amid a chorus of loud cheers and applause from both crews. From there, we were in tow for the three hundred miles to Okinawa's Buchner Bay where we would wait out the storm.

By the greatest of good fortune, Bobby, my early-childhood, copper-boiler-bathtub kid brother, was a gunner's mate on the USS *Tuscaloosa*! We had not seen each other since we went our separate ways after my high school graduation two years earlier.

I persuaded my commanding officer to commandeer a small landing craft as soon as we settled down in Buchner Bay. After hightailing it to Bobby's heavy cruiser, Dr. Burgess visited with the medical officers while I hustled to the fantail. I jumped into Bobby's gunwale, surprising him so that he half turned his 20mm anti-aircraft gun on me. It was a throat-choking, teary-eyed reunion never to be forgotten a half-century down the road.

Alive and Well

I wondered once more, and not for the last time, what I was doing there, what we were all doing. Ah, yes, it was for our country--to protect it from foreign aggression, to preserve it for our parents and siblings, for our loved ones, for future generations.

When I had been in the friendly harbors of the Hawaiian Islands a few weeks prior to that event, the question had not seemed so urgent. It had not involved thoughts of life and death. The beautiful waters there, for many miles around, had been filled with ships of all kinds as they awaited fleet assignment to the war zone.

The enormity of the cost of that mighty armada was also a baffling thought. I found it no less difficult to understand the magnitude of our current national debt. For me, it was akin to trying to conceive the infinity of the universe!

Entering the military service in those days was expected. After graduating from high school at five feet four inches tall, and weighing in at one hundred twenty pounds, I figured I wouldn't have made much of a United States Marine, and the thought of carrying sixty pounds of pack on my back had discouraged me from joining the Army. Therefore, I had convinced myself that the Navy would be the place for me. Young and naive, my fellow male graduates and I had headed promptly for the recruiting office. Popularized by a catchy tune of the time, those "bell-bottom trousers" and "a coat of Navy blue" had enticed me to become a sailor.

At times, I was very pleased with my decision, for there were days of great beauty and serenity sailing the seas of the South Pacific. With their mirror-like surfaces, blue skies, and warm, balmy days, it is no wonder that they proved to be a tropical inspiration for the Broadway musical that would one day commemorate our affair. Clear nights comforted me, for I knew that I shared those same twinkling stars and bright full moon with the ones I loved halfway around the world.

Most days were average, beginning with early wake-up at daybreak. Routines were not unlike those in the lives of people who remained on the home front. Medical personnel had particular assignments such as x-ray, lab testing, patient care, sick call, record keeping, and dental care. Occasionally, minor injury treatment was required. Now and then, an appendectomy had to be performed. And regularly, there were battle station exercises.

Entertainment was a once-in-a-while movie projected onto a large screen on the main deck. Personal visits by Hollywood celebrities were unheard of. The USO was only a combination of three letters in the alphabet. Radio, newspapers, and music were not on our agenda except for regular broadcasts from Radio Japan. The sweet, pleasant voice of Tokyo Rose was heard with nostalgic all-American music in the background. Rosie claimed we were losing the war. Constantly, she urged us to stop fighting, to give up, so we could go back to friends and loved ones.

News from home by way of radio and releases was denied us. Someone at the top had decided we were better off not knowing what was going on in the outside world. We had to depend on personal mail; but, in a war zone, letters were few and far between. Every few months an official mail ship managed to find us.

Mail call was both a happy and a sad event. Each time our yeoman announced it over the loud speaker, there was a stampede to midship, where we scrunched around the mail carrier who was bellowing out one name after another. It was not unusual to be called several times or not at all. Either way, each of us retreated to our own quiet corner, with or without letters from home.

Concern about enemy submarines lurking in the waters beneath us became no more than a casual thought. It was something we pushed below our consciousness where it remained as an unspoken worry. It did help some to realize that a torpedo, properly fired, would be a very sudden event. Periodic oil slicks and cauldrons of air bubbles in the passing waters were brief reminders that other ships had fallen victim to an enemy submarine not so far away or so long ago.

The Country Doctor

After the Japanese surrender in September of 1944, the *Colbert* became one in a fleet of warships and carriers that transported occupation troops to Korea. Our entry into the harbor at Darien, on the southern tip of the peninsula was, indeed, a triumphant one. Several miles out, we were met by a flotilla of small boats with highly decorated sails. They were crammed with people jubilant to be liberated from years of Japanese military oppression. It was a holiday spectacle that ended with the awesome task of taking on 500 American Prisoners of War who had survived the death march of Bataan and Corrigidor, where the Japanese had defeated the U.S. forces in 1942. The men had managed to survive three years of internment in a Manchurian prison camp, and we were there to take them home!

As a significant-sized transport vessel, we were well equipped to do the job. Our large sick bay served as the hospital for prisoners ravaged by malnutrition and a variety of infected wounds. It was an easy switch from receiving casualties from island, beach-head assaults in Okinawa to taking our own prisoners of internment home again.

Sadly, three of them never made it. They were standing on deck leaning on the ship's rail right where the mine had exploded. Two of them were killed outright. The third suffered a severe head injury, and his tragedy

8

Alive and Well

consumed us for three days. Two other corpsman and myself rotated through seventy-two hours of constant vigil. Frequent checking of his vital signs and unrelenting artificial respiration turned us into a human ventilator unit. It lasted until all hope for his recovery was gone and the ship's surgeon reluctantly pronounced him dead.

I have to admit that three months on a dead ship is ninety days akin to the *Rime of the Ancient Mariner* experience. To be without power for cooking, lighting, and cold storage is to be a floating hobo, reaching for handouts from occasional passing ships. Three months of eating powdered eggs, milk, and ham in cans marked SPAM® was difficult to swallow.

The first fruit we received after more than sixty days was a shipment of cantaloupe in crates. It never reached the storage area below deck. The ship's crew decided it would keep better in hungry bellies than in the hot, humid compartments down under. It was the first and only time I've seen a melon peeled, drained of its seeds, and eaten like an apple. That melon has been the apple of my eye to this day. I have never had a tastier one since. And fifty years later, I still can't look a SPAM® can in the label.

When the curtain of the war closed with the holocaust of nuclear bombs over Nagasaki and Hiroshima, my itinerary took me from the Yellow Sea to Okinawa, then on to Guam, where my ship was decommissioned.

The Country Doctor

The entire crew was transferred to other ships in the South Pacific. My lot was to go to Yokohama and then to Tokyo where I was living witness to war's devastation. Cities were flattened to the ground by B-29 bombs and battleship cannons. Pathetic little, one-room, scrap-metal shacks were the beginning of postwar Japanese reconstruction.

On my way back to the United States, I was a passenger on an oil tanker. It had been in the Pacific area to supply warships with battle-ready fuel. Being a pharmacist's mate, I was privileged to live in the small sick bay for the twenty-one days it took to travel from Tokyo Bay around the Arctic Circle to San Francisco.

The ship's medical officer was a lazy, unkempt, overweight, shaggy-headed man who spent those entire three weeks wondering whether he would ever be able to successfully re-enter the peace-time medical profession. He gave me cause to wonder what he ever amounted to before the war. Nevertheless, he was the inspiration that rekindled my smoldering desire to become a physician. I decided during the trip that I wanted to, knew I could, had to, become a physician in order to help save the American people from a lost-cause doctor like him. I was to be reminded later on that even in a profession like medicine, there can be failures and misfits.

Alive and Well

Five typhoons, a crippled ship, dozens of oil slicks, six beach-head assaults, two nuclear bombs, and two years later, I sailed under the San Francisco Bay Bridge, then headed east to Pennsylvania as fast as I could get there.

I was on my way.

> *One of the nicest things about the future is that it comes one day at a time.*

Interlude 1

Anxiety

Anxiety is a naturally occurring requirement for membership in the human race. Early man experienced it when chased by the saber-toothed tiger in savannahs of long ago. We experience it today while nuclear bombs dangle over our heads.

Symptoms of anxiety include one or more of the following: palpitation, poor concentration, shortness of breath, dizziness, queasiness, sweating, weakness, and shakiness. Some combination of these symptoms causes you to want to run, if you can, or stay and fight, if you must.

To be occasionally anxious then is to be normal. It is when anxiety is sudden, severe, frequent, or associated with depression that your ongoing well-being is affected and normal life and normal living are no longer possible.

Sometimes, we can handle anxiety on our own; at other times, it may require the help of others. Treatment may include the temporary use of prescription medication and psychotherapy of one kind or another. Counseling with your doctor, minister, psychologist, or psychiatrist is sometimes necessary. Don't depend on a family member or a friend. They may be very caring but not objective enough to be significantly helpful.

Chapter 2

Cake Walk

Laughter is a pressure valve that keeps you from exploding.

Growing up in the socially depressed years of the 1920's, the third-born in a family of nine, where the first child was a boy and the second a girl, meant I was not number one. I was neither first boy nor first girl. I was definitely number three and the smallest of the bunch to boot. That added up to a big challenge for me from the moment of my birth.

And yet, I have vivid memories of frequent pats on my head, accompanied by parental and other adult exclamations of, "Oh, isn't he a good, cute, little boy?"

"You are not number one," three times over, and, "You're a good, cute, little boy," were powerful messages that channeled my possible direction in life. Throughout my formative years, they were constantly reinforced by playmates and school chums, relatives, and teachers.

When I was in high school, I had wanted to play basketball and football. I could never qualify for competition in high and broad jumps. I was always last in college gym classes when two classmate captains selected team mates for volley ball.

However, I rejected the message that I did not measure up, that I didn't fit. According to my way of thinking, it was they who did not fit me.

Somewhere along the way, I made the decision to be number one at something in spite of my birth slot. It began with falling in love with simple things. I was in an ideal spot for it to happen--a small town in the country, a large family in the early 1900's. I had wonderful childhood experiences and fond memories. My incubator was an abiding appreciation for the natural world right in my own back yard.

Acceptance of, rather than resignation to, my shortcomings and my size, somehow enabled me to transform the negative elements of my life into positive ones. Today, deep retrospection has enlightened me that it was my mother who enabled this to happen. Her own special way of accepting life's adversities, with a nine-child family, with a verbally-abusive mate, in the economically-depressed early twentieth century, became the foundation of my own development.

Times were difficult, and my mother needed help when I was born. For three months I was my mother's and my black nanny's baby, and that meant a lot of holding and hugging and loving.

Alive and Well

A nanny, you know, can give a new human baby a very positive start in life. I know Aunty Jewel did for me. She was from one of the several black families in my little Allegheny Mountain hometown. Her kids and I were schoolmates for twelve years, and through it all, none of us experienced prejudice. I had to leave home seventeen years later for the wide world outside Central Pennsylvania to realize there was such a thing.

Fifty years and more ago, most families were well-peopled with children. Four or five made up a small family. Eight or ten were average. A dozen or more were a big group. Birth control and family planning were as unknown as women's liberation. In my own family, a new child was born about every eighteen to twenty-four months over a period of eighteen years. Birth control, therefore, was pretty well guaranteed during nine months of pregnancy aided by a few months or so of breastfeeding in between.

It was also the case that (with my family of nine children) as the last several were born, the first few were leaving home on their way to a job, school, or military service. For the few years all nine were still under the same roof, we were two psychosocially different groups.

Those were the days when girls were given old-time double names that stayed with them for a lifetime: Mary Alice and Rose Marie and Betty Jane and the like.

The Country Doctor

Nicknames were unheard of, and each time someone was addressed by anyone in or outside the family, it was by way of the complete double name. It left no doubt in anybody's mind who was being called.

Simplicity back then meant being bathed in a copper boiler with my brother Bobby when, at ages one and three, we were both still small enough to fit into it together. In canning season during the summer and fall, the copper boiler hot-packed fruits and vegetables for winter fare. At all other times, it was our bath tub with water all the way up to our chins.

Simplicity also meant family reunions at a time when getting together was annual, and a very big social event. In the 1920's, families were big, travel was uncommon, relatives most often lived within a few miles or so, and a picnic was well attended by four generations-- especially at meal time.

The group photo was two to three feet long and about one foot high so that four tiers of people could be included. The picture was taken by the Brownie box camera from far enough away to get everyone in. We were identified by a name beneath the picture. Our faces were not very well defined. The trick was to match the name with the face. As the years passed, more pieces of the puzzle became lost in the fading memories of increasingly fewer survivors.

Alive and Well

Simplicity further meant cake walks in the gentle summertime. Back then, they were the big social event in small rural towns and were held every Friday night. The movie house was open on Saturday nights only, and radio was for weekdays and Sundays.

Bert, the local fiddler, made music for the affair. At times, his tempo was more like a quadrille than a walk. Couples, hand in hand, strolled and skipped around a 100-foot square of grass in the middle of the town's one-block park. Cakes sat on pedestals in each corner. When the music stopped, the couple nearest the cake took the prize home for Sunday dinner. And so it went for two hours until all the cakes were gone. As soon as it was over, the village ladies began their baking projects for the following week.

A cake walk was the one occasion in a week's time that young men looked their dressy best and the girls looked their loveliest. Although I was too young, I surely did yearn to be among those pretty young ladies.

On the other hand, I didn't always like girls--especially girls with long hair, and most especially if it was a ponytail or an extra long double pigtail.

I remember being five years old and in first grade. The elementary school in my home town of Curwensville, population three thousand, contained grades one through five and ten through twelve. I never questioned why the

The Country Doctor

other four were in another building a half mile away on the other side of town. It may have had to do with space. The first and second grades were in the same room. There were twenty first graders on one side and twenty second graders on the other. Big, husky Mrs. Ratstetter was definitely in charge of both classes. With crossed arms resting on her very ample bosom and both index fingers pointing straight ahead, no one ever questioned that.

Since my last name began with "H" and Chrissy's started with "K," alphabetical order put me right behind her, in the second seat from the front, on the extreme left side of the room, directly in front of the teacher's desk. It came out that way when the teacher started with the letter "A" in the last seat in the back.

It may have been highly circumstantial that I was always placed near the front of the room during my elementary school years. I sometimes wondered whether it was because of my short stature. It made it easier for me to see the blackboard. It also made it easier for the teacher to keep a close eye on me. And it put Crissy's pigtails right in front of my face, with the ends dangling on top of my desk, right beside my inkwell, filled with blue-black ink.

Now, what's a young boy to do? It just naturally happened that Crissy's pigtails occasionally wound up in my inkwell. As soon as they did, I would look around for a place to hide. And that was very difficult to do when I was in the second seat from the front, in the presence of a screaming girl, with thirty-eight pairs of eyes looking right at the two of us. Those were the times when I became acquainted with a high wooden stool that sat in the right-hand corner at the front of the room.

Every now and then Mrs. Ratstetter asked me to sit on that stool for a while. The grim look on her face and her long, pointed finger showed me the way. A strange-looking pointed white hat sat on my head while I perched on the stool. Years later, I realized that my experiences in the corner were the inspiration for my love affair with hats and the collections I gathered along the way.

I was proud to be there in that corner. There I was with my special view of the whole class. I could see all thirty-nine fellow pupils in the room, and they could see me. It was definitely the best front-row seat in the entire schoolhouse. It was very nice to see them occasionally laugh at me from behind their hands or books while I smiled right back at them.

Mrs. Ratstetter's first and second grades gave me a good start in life. One of the things that came naturally to me was ham acting. It began when I was occasionally caught talking out of turn with Kenny, a nearby fellow pupil. The reward for this was another Ratstetter invitation to stand in front of the class with my friend and

The Country Doctor

sing a song for our classmates. It would take a few minutes for us to agree on what to sing. I'll never forget our favorite, "There's a Shanty in Old Shanty Town." I don't seem to remember our audience applauding us all that much for our rendition, but, it did get us a lot of laughs.

My dislike for girls didn't last too long. As I got older, I was quick to learn there was more to girls than hair and pigtails--especially when it crowned the head of a beautiful, blue-eyed, blond-haired princess.

*If you haven't got a sense of humor,
you've got no sense at all.*

Interlude 2

Some Quick Fixes

To relieve the pain of blisters, snip off a small sliver at the edge and press the fluid out. Keep it covered with paper tape for two to three days. It will be more comfortable and heal faster, too.

A build-up of callouses on the feet can be painful. They can be self-treated by using fine sandpaper or an emery board as often as necessary. This is much safer than paring with a knife or a sharp blade. The callouses must be dry in order to accomplish the task.

The discomfort and nuisance of mouth ulcers can be minimized by placing an aspirin tablet on the site until the aspirin dissolves. A few seconds of momentary increase in pain can save you days of pain afterwards. The ulcer will heal quicker as well.

Chapter 3

Fetal Physician

Childishness is one thing; childlikeness is quite another.

The switch had just been turned to "ON" by the labor-room nurse, and before the light had actually illuminated the room, I was wide awake and hightailing it to Delivery Room Number One to bring the first baby of my twelve-month rotating internship into its new world.

It is like that when one is on call for the obstetrical service. A switch clicks on, the eyelids snap open, then the light comes on. It was a very rapid series of events that vaulted me out of bed as I raced to the Delivery Room to arrive before the baby did! I almost always made it.

It took no time at all to get dressed, since I slept in the scrub suit that I also wore all day. The only accuracy necessary was to hit the floor running into my shoes. That was my twenty-four-hour uniform during the twelve months of internship. When internship was over, it felt strange to wear regular clothes again.

"Wow!" I had said to my fellow interns. "I really lucked out! What a way to start out a year's worth of hospital training between medical school and medical practice!"

I had chosen the obstetrical service intentionally, thinking it so symbolic as a beginning for my training and new life for babies. There was something poetic about that. It meant delivering babies for two months and rotating on the gynecology service at the same time. It seemed fitting to learn about the diseases, illnesses, and health of both mother and child at the same time.

It hadn't occurred to me that obstetrics meant night calls (when the majority of babies are born). That added up to a twenty-four-hour day, sometimes for two or three days in a row.

I could not have chosen a more exciting way to start. By the end of the first night, day number one of rapid transition from student to experiential doctor, I had six notches on my delivery stick. At the end of two months, after notching off number one hundred, there was no room left on the stick. The actual number of trips to the delivery room was ninety-eight, for twice I simultaneously delivered babies from two different mothers on adjoining delivery tables.

The challenge of delivering a baby safely--for mother, child, and doctor--can be so intense that it is easy to become lost in the technique of the task and miss the beauty and the miracle of new life.

The Country Doctor

In years to come, the miracle would return when I stood by the delivery table watching the specialist do the delivery while I, as a family doctor/pediatrician, was there to accept and examine the newborn and make sure a precious and delicate life was able to continue breathing.

Hearing a loud cry after the initial pat on the buns is an essential part of the miracle, but I decided early on that slapping the newborn child on the bare bottom is a cruel introduction to life. It is enough of a shock to leave the cozy confines of a floating waterbed and be squeezed through a tight birth canal into the cold, outside world. It's no wonder a tender and sensitive little one sometimes develops a complex about spanking.

The transition from the gentle confines of a mother's womb, where baby is comforted in a warm-water world and frequent pats through the abdomen, programs a new life for petting and hugging. It is a joy initiated at the time of the child's conception, when mother's egg takes in and embraces father's sperm. It is, also, a need, strongly reinforced by a snug squeeze through the birth canal. It seems shameful to spank its new-born bottom the moment the baby enters the outside world. A brisk rub up and down the spine does the trick just as well.

I was not a total novice on my first day of internship, however. I had already delivered twenty-five babies while on hospital obstetrical service in medical school. Things were different as an intern, though. I was intimately and intensely involved in the birth process, more on my own, with a higher degree of responsibility. It would have been the worst possible place to make a mistake.

Easing the baby out of the birth canal as soon as the tip of its head appeared was priority number one. At delivery number ninety-eight, it was still as important as it had been with the first.

Priority number two was to minimize the tearing of the mother's surrounding tissue, since a baby's head often seems to be about five times larger than its exit. Despite the most careful attention to massaging the vaginal rim around an increasingly-protruding baby, it was sometimes necessary to make an incision. In certain cases it was imperative to prevent uncontrollable tearing which could cause serious injury to the mother's rectum and bladder.

As soon as the baby was born, breathing, and freed of its umbilical cord, priority number three was to carefully suture the mother's wound so that excessive scarring would not result in future discomfort and difficult childbirths. Depending on the needs of the baby and the necessity to minimize tissue tearing, the size of the incisions varied. At times, they had to be deep and long.

It took another half hour to put things back together. During the process, I often wondered how Dr. Eberhart, of some 35 years ago, had been able to perform

The Country Doctor

such a miracle in my mother's bedroom. Of course, I knew that the process had become quicker and easier after Mother had delivered several of my siblings. By the time the ninth one came, she was able to do it herself with only the help of a neighbor.

A few years later, it was unheard of for a baby to be born at home. Except for those few who had to be delivered by distraught fathers, taxi drivers, and firemen along the way, they all went to the hospital whether they needed to or not. Hospital deliveries were said to be safer for both mother and child. They were definitely more convenient for the doctor. And, they became increasingly more expensive.

It wasn't until some thirty years later that the pendulum began its swing in the opposite direction. Baby-boomer parents of the 60's and 70's became increasingly interested in the options of natural childbirth and home delivery.

As expected, the conservative colleagues in my medical community would not hear of anything so unconventional. It took one obstetrician and myself to promote the idea. After our first several deliveries--all successful because of our own careful selectiveness and diligent attention--the movement was underway. Parents continued to exert mounting pressure on the medical establishment. It was an issue that was not about to be ignored.

The medical community compromised by developing the birthing room at hospitals. A woman in labor could be admitted just in time for hospitalized delivery in the most natural way possible. The father was no longer excluded or expected to pace the corridor. Instead he was right there by the delivery table along with the pediatrician. When everything went well, the proud parents and the newborn child could leave the hospital for home after a few hours or so. My friend and I had opened the Birthing Room delivery door.

It was fitting that my pediatric service rotation followed obstetrics and gynecology. I became intimately acquainted with infants and children, both healthy and diseased. I was able to watch the growth of babies I had delivered just two months before. Occasionally, I helped feed the young ones and sometimes rocked them to sleep after finishing my intern duties for the day. It was easy to fall in love with them. It was, also, easy to fall asleep with them still in my arms after I would sing my own version of:

Rock-a-bye baby, in the treetop.
When the wind blows, the cradle will rock.
And if the bough breaks, sweet baby will fall
Into my arms, safe and sound after all.

With increasing mellowness in my own mind and heart, I decided the fairy tales and nursery rhymes of elder days were terrible for babies and young children. During their most impressionable years, they were rocked to sleep and put to bed with visions of wolves eating young girls, pigs boiling wolves to death, and stepmothers poisoning pretty little girls with bright red apples. I've often wanted to rewrite them all.

On the other hand, in today's world of violence, wickedness, and greed, and with an overload of low moral psychosocial behavior in all people "great" and "small," could it be that the authors of fairy tales and nursery rhymes back then knew what they were doing after all? Perhaps they had the foresight to desensitize and prepare us for the crazy present.

The moment I met Becky, she became one of my favorite patients and persons. Becky first entered the hospital while I was still on the pediatric service. She was very sick with what turned out to be a case of nephrosis of the kidneys. Only vaguely did I realize or want to think about the gravity of her disease back then in the 1950's.

That ideally beautiful four-year-old child, blessed with an equally captivating personality, was plagued with the immense problem of repeated attacks of kidney failure. Her sweetly innocent life was doomed to an early end.

Becky entered the back pages of my mind over the following six months as I rotated through internal medicine, surgery, neurology, and other specialty fields.

She returned in stark reality during the last month of my internship on the pathology service. I entered the autopsy room one day to see her precious little body on the cold stone autopsy table, awaiting my help with her postmortem examination. In all the years since, she has never left my mind.

At that moment, I didn't feel all that fortunate. I began my internship bringing life into the world and ended it by seeing some of those lives leaving.

A twin birth is an infant replay.

Interlude 3

Insomnia

It has been said by "the experts" that some thirty million people in the United States have trouble sleeping each night. That figure includes those who have difficulty falling to sleep, those who awaken frequently, those plagued by nightmares, and those who sleep so lightly that the drop of an eyelash would awaken them.

Decide for yourself whether or not you have insomnia. Don't take it from someone else who wants to sell you a sleeping pill or a new mattress or advise you to replace your sleeping partner with one who does not snore.

If you feel reasonably well rested during the day and you're reasonably able to accomplish all that you choose to do, physically and mentally, you are getting enough rest.

Chapter 4

Big George

*Be careful about following directions,
you might just end up where you're not going.*

"Who is this?" I asked, a little surprised to hear a young boy's voice at the other end of the line in the middle of a school day. "Is your Mom home?"

"It's Little George," he answered. "I'll get her."

Wednesday afternoons have become a time for my regular four-hour, eighty-mile, house-call rounds. The trip includes several calls in Susquehoning and other stops in the surrounding countryside, in all directions, as far away as twenty miles.

The dozen or so patients I see are all homebound because of advanced illness or age. Some of them suffer from terminal cancer, stroke, heart disease, cerebral palsy, or Alzheimer's disease. Their ages range up to ninety-seven years.

Jane got on the line and explained, "It's George, Doc. He just got back in from a milk association meeting in

The Country Doctor

Denver, and he's really sick. He can't get out of bed. Can you come out?"

The image of Big George was taking shape in my mind as I listened to Jane. George was a man with a laugh as big as his frame, and he could fill a doorway with no trouble at all. It would have taken an ambulance with a full crew to get him in to me or to the hospital, 35 miles away.

"I'll be out that way on calls this afternoon. You can expect me then," I promised.

By early afternoon, I manipulated my old, four-wheel-drive pickup, Chunker, off the asphalt secondary onto a muddy road that sloped down into a shallow valley just outside the village of Goosetown.

Vehicles of the vintage of my old truck are called clunkers, but not mine. Mine is built with a broad wheel base, slung low to the road, with tires that grab the ground and hang on for dear life. It refuses to be turned over. Yet, under the right combination of circumstances, it is willing enough to get stuck in the mud or snow. More than a few times we have been towed out of drifts and ditches and fields by the closest farm tractor or plow horse.

My truck chugs along the road at pretty much its own pace, regardless of the gearage, eating up the miles one chunk at a time. There are a lot of clunkers out there, but mine is the only Chunker I know.

As I drove down the winding road to the Williams Farm, I once again appreciated the wonderful Allegheny Mountains. Surrounding me was the most beautiful deciduous mountain country, a year-round sporting arena for hunting and fishing, and a treasure chest for the nature photographer, writer, and outdoor person.

Hills and valleys and fields and streams have become the picture frames of my reference, wildflowers and wildlife my companions. At any time of the year, my senses are filled with the magic and mystery of the mountains and its people.

I dodged some white-tailed deer on my journey, and one wayward cow. All the while, the slopes of the mountains reinforced my sense of everlasting at-homeness.

"Our road is exactly one mile past the village general store," Jane had told me. "Look for a wooden shelter on the left at the top of the hill where the boys wait for the school bus. Turn right, onto our road, and come down the slope exactly one-half mile. Look for a white frame house on the left with a red barn right across the way. There is a sign right there that has our name on it."

Now, I have become very careful about directions to country places over the years, especially when the word

The Country Doctor

"exactly" is used before the number of miles. Many times, both day and night, I have found myself lost. Country nights can be very dark, and the back roads are lightly traveled. The distance between me and a dusk-to-dawn light can be a lot of miles to go.

As Jane finished her directions with a confident, "You can't miss it," I found myself thinking about my first house call several years ago to Clara Piper's place.

"Turn right by the green Esso service station. You can't miss it, Doc." What Clara hadn't told me was that the service station had recently changed hands to Sunoco. Also, the station's color had changed from green to white. Sure enough, I missed it.

With Jane's directions fresh in my mind, I drove off the ridge down into a shallow, windswept valley that resembled of the lower half of a wind tunnel. The directions were scribbled on my prescription pad so I wouldn't forget a turn or a landmark. Most of the time, I remember to bring the pad.

The Chunker and I slid down the wet, muddy surface aided by a strong gust of wind. With careful aim, I managed to stay on the road until it leveled off a bit. Slowly and cautiously, I accelerated onward, grateful that it was not an icy road of winter. Three miles passed and I had yet to see "The Williams Farm" sign, although I did see several white houses with red barns across the way.

Alive and Well

As I turned around to try it from the other direction, I was certain I heard the Chunker chuckling. So many times the grill of my old friend takes on the appearance of a laughing face with its bumper twisted into a smirk.

Two and a half miles back up the road, I stopped at one of the many red barns. Stepping out of the Chunker, I yelled over the roar of the farmer's tractor motor and asked directions to the Williams Farm.

"You're on it!" he shouted back.

The sign was nowhere to be seen as I felt the icy sting of the wind strip away what little warmth my clothing gave me. I looked down to see my shoes buried in mud to the shoe strings and said, "Yep, and it looks like I am *in* it, too. Where do I find Big George?"

He pointed to the back door of the house across the way.

I had to hold onto my hat to keep it on my head. I was thankful for the black bag in my other hand, for its weight kept me from blowing away like the Williams Farm sign.

Inside the Williams' home, the wind whistled in and around the windows with a musical note I had not heard since the summers I had spent on my grandfather's farm long ago and far away among the Pennsylvania hills of

Clinton County. I was momentarily overwhelmed by the pleasant ghostliness of a nostalgic past.

I imagined I was back in the kitchen of that old farmhouse. It was dark outside. My older brother and I sat with my grandmother and grandfather, talking together by the light of a kerosene lamp. At age six years, I was homesick for my family a hundred miles away.

During the day, Chuck and I helped mow hay with a pair of horses. There was no such thing as a tractor. Wheat and oats were cut to the ground with a scythe, something I was not big enough to use. I did help make sheaves after the cutting, though.

The trick was to gather up an armful and then tie it together with a half dozen or so strands of stalk. A dozen of these bundles were then stacked together until the whole field was harvested. Horses and wagons were driven through the rows to load the shocks destined for the barn. There, on the main floor, each bundle was threshed by hand to separate the grain from the stem. Grain ended up in a bin for later use as food for livestock and flour for the kitchen. Stems became straw bedding for cows, horses, and chickens.

I decided that farmhouses such as those would have made great little sanitariums for tuberculosis patients of earlier days when fresh air and sunshine in season were

Alive and Well

the only treatment around. It was a pleasant country environment, and Jane told me how nice and cool it was in the summertime.

I found Big George in his country-cool bedroom buried under an even bigger mountain of country quilts. I knew he was in there somewhere from the clouds of water vapor that hovered over an opening near the topmost blanket. Ordinarily he would not have consented to a house call. In fact, he likely would not admit that he needed medical care at all. I was there only because Jane had summoned me and because he was truly sick with the fever and cough and the aches and pains of a severe case of bronchitis.

There are many rugged individuals like Big George here in my part of the world. Nine times out of ten they are men. They are not at all unlike those of older times and similar places. Today's breed may be more educated, more successful, and more affluent. Yet deep inside their soul, that old trait of imaginary indestructibility still glimmers through.

Big George was happy enough to see me that day after all. He was too weak to complain and unable to resist the penicillin shot destined for his bare backside. He even agreed to stay in the house and take it easy for the following three days, giving up a business trip to New England and his work in the barn and fields. It would be

The Country Doctor

very unlike George, but he decided he was sick enough to cooperate with Jane and me at the moment.

"You know this all started out as the flu, George," I reminded him. "When fall comes, you should think about getting the vaccine. We have had the flu vaccine for quite a few years," I said, "and it's one of the best we've ever had."

"Does it work?" Jane asked.

"It can prevent the flu that occurs from mid-December to the first part of March for about eighty-five percent of those who take it," I replied, "and for the other fifteen percent, the symptoms will be mild. Another good reason for taking it is to prevent complications such as bronchitis and pneumonia."

Looking like a big black bear settling in for hibernation, Big George grumbled and moaned under his breath as he slid back under the quilts; I was not at all sure he would consent to a shot come October or November. But I did know, at that moment, he wished he had taken the vaccine the previous year.

As I descended the creaky steps of that simple, yet solid, hundred-year-old farmhouse, I realized how typical it was of its place in time, occupied with only the necessary furnishings and furniture.

Alive and Well

"This house has character," I reflected, "a personality. It feels like an old friend." I walked away from the Williams Farm, not all that anxious to leave.

My Chunker's climb to the top of the ridge took longer than its slippery descent of an hour before. We stopped there for a while looking down over the valley--the white house, the red barn, the cows in the meadows, and the fields that were ready for corn and wheat. The scene was frame-worked by fence rows and woodlands. Days of youth flashed before me and filled me with sweet nostalgia.

I reminisced for a while about boyhood summertimes in the month of June when huckleberries were at the peak of tasty-blue ripeness. Early morning hikes to the berry patches, sometimes several miles away, took my brothers and me into the hills with pails in hand and lunch in pocket, eager to fill the buckets--but not for the love of picking berries. The joy of swimming in the pristine water of a cool mountain stream was our inspiration. It seemed uncanny that berry patches were always located near the ol' swimming holes and that the pails were filled at the time of the day's greatest heat and humidity.

Country boys did not know of tractors back then. We, also, did not own swim suits. Skinny-dipping was the

The Country Doctor

only way to go. In the heat and humidity of a berry-picking day, there was no greater pleasure. Picking was quick, swimming was long, and summers were all too short. No wonder they went so fast; like dream fragments of so much more that is remembered less and less.

*I would have come to see you last week, Doctor,
but I wasn't well enough.*

Interlude 4

Whatisitis?

Whatisitis is not a disease. It is a question: what is -itis?

The answer is that -itis is a suffix found at the end of many medical words. For example, there is appendicitis, sinusitis, and bursitis.

It means inflammation of the kind of tissue that precedes it in the word. Therefore, tendinitis means inflammation of the tendon.

Inflammation comes about because of some kind of irritation. Irritation may be brought about by bumps, cuts, scrapes, over-stretching or overuse of muscles and tendons, or by tearing a ligament. Hence, there are words such as fibrositis, myositis, and epicondylitis.

Irritation can, also, come about because of some disease in the body that focuses on certain types of parts and organs. In this group of conditions are such things as arthritis, arteritis, and thyroiditis.

Viruses and bacteria, too, can cause irritation of certain parts of the body such as the mucous membranes

The Country Doctor

of the respiratory tract, so that we speak of rhinitis, laryngitis, and bronchitis.

Chemicals in foods can cause irritation. Thus, there are conditions called gastritis, colitis, and cystitis.

The symptoms of -itis are swelling, pain, tenderness, and heat. The latter explains why an arthritic joint may feel hot to the touch and why we experience fever with a cold or sore throat.

When an -itis condition is mild and you know with certainty what it is, it can be treated by resting, by not moving or using that part of the body. Many of them can also be helped by cold compresses. Additional relief can be achieved by taking a medication, such as acetaminophen and ibuprofen, to counteract the inflammation.

When conditions are more painful than you can tolerate or treat by yourself, it is time to see your doctor. The doctor will diagnose the condition and, if required, treat you for inflammation, pain, and the underlying cause. What is used will depend on the cause and severity of your own particular -itis.

And that's what -itis is.

Chapter 5

Say Ahhh

Many little things add up to one big lot.

Next to food, shelter, and clothing, it is the little things that mean a lot for human life and living.

Paper clips, staples, and safety pins are important, of course. And what would we do without rubber bands, Q-Tips®, and toothpicks? But it is a flat, six-inch little piece of wood, 1/16" thick and rounded at both ends, that takes first prize. Perhaps it's because the tongue depressor is such a simple, inexpensive thing with universal versatility. And, it's safe.

Paper clips can get complicated with their different sizes and shapes. They also have a special capacity for getting infernally tangled with each other. To reach for one and get a dozen or more in the form of a 12-inch chain or a bunch the size of a golf ball is a frequent frustration for me. On the other hand, I remember how well a rubber band between the thumb and index finger loaded with a clip could shoot out the light bulb in Mrs. Ratstetter's second-grade classroom. A paper wad against her backside while she faced the chalkboard got her

The Country Doctor

attention as well. And staples are a bane to bare feet on a rug. It's not uncommon for them to clip fingers together and, along with safety pins and paper clips, find their way into throats, lungs, and intestinal tracts of adults and children alike.

And who can forget the paper airplane, the e-mail of the classroom in the 1930's, readily made by the proper folds of an 8½" by 11½" sheet of paper and launched by the proper twist of the wrist. It would sail through the air with the greatest of ease, carrying fun messages to friends and notes to puppy loves. The trick was to get it to the right receiver, especially unnoticed by Mrs. Ratstetter's eyes-in-the-back-of-the-head radar. It worked about ten percent of the time. With the other ninety percent, the sender stood at the front of the room and read the message to the entire class.

For many of us, the tongue depressor was one of the first doctor tools to which we were introduced as infants, along with the stethoscope. Both were memorable. The stick tasted so bland, and the scope felt so cold.

The original tongue depressor was invented to depress the tongue--to press it down out of the way in order to get a good look at the tonsils and throat.

It takes a definite amount of firm and steady pressure to hold the tongue at bay. Each time the doctor asks you to open up, it is the tongue's nature to rear up like a single-humped camel. It's a formidable hump at that, since it is ninety-five percent muscle and a tough one, too. It has to be, considering the way it is used for eating and talking.

My acquaintance with this wonderful instrument was lost after my infancy. I was a healthy child and adolescent. It was not until premedical school days that we found each other again. At that time, it became a stirring rod for cream and sugar in the coffee cup. As a biology major taking many lengthy lab courses, I found it was necessary to have a coffee break two or three times during a session. In the decade of the 1940's, my classmates and I established the original coffee club, and the tongue depressor became a mark of personal uniqueness. Our white china cups took on a tannish-stained pattern that identified each of us as surely as a handwritten signature. So, too, did our tongue depressors. There was no doubt about which cup and which stick belonged to whom. The stain pattern seemed to take on the personality of the owner.

As medical school advanced to the patient care stage, my relationship with the tongue depressor became more intimate and intense. It was a constant companion in the pocket of my intern scrub shirt, along with a writing pen, a flashlight, and the end of the stethoscope. The latter was put there to keep it out of the patient's face

The Country Doctor

during examination and out of the soup bowl at meal time. It, also, kept it out of the fly of my pants after a hasty exit from the bathroom.

It was the tongue depressor which proved the most useful of all the simple, little possessions in the ongoing life of a fledgling physician. It served me in so many ways and so well. It became a knife, fork, or spoon; a spreader of jellies and jams, peanut and apple butter; and an applicator of glue and paste.

It was a scraper for all manner of sticky things on all kinds of surfaces. It won't scratch metal or glass. It served me as a wedge, a filler of cracks, and a leveler of tables and chairs and writing surfaces. It made a dandy bookmark for endless nights of study.

It could be used as a screwdriver, a prop (either end to end or side to side to hold doors and windows open and to keep them from rattling in the wind), or an insect swatter (by holding one end firmly and snapping the other down on a wayward fly). A splintered one could plug up holes or serve as a toothpick. The tongue depressor cut up pizza and leveled Christmas trees.

"Say ahhh," I said to Rosie as I was about to examine her throat. I no more than pointed the tongue depressor in the direction of her face than her mouth

Alive and Well

snapped open as though I had pressed a button marked "Open Wide."

Now, a patient's response to the doctor's request to "Say ahhh" is a very personal thing, as unique as the individual's personality. Sometimes it is a passive response whereby the mouth is opened slowly into a slit about the width of the tongue depressor's thickness. Other times, there is a casual yawn-type response. Another response is a quick, cavernous opening with all teeth showing like that of an angry animal. Another resembles a smile, and still another, as though the patient is in pain.

Some "ahhhs" are little round holes, others horizontal, and others vertical slits. Some patients hide their teeth by tightening the lips while others expose all thirty-two, a very long tongue, and both tonsils.

Background sounds such as grunts, groans, hums, squeals, squeaks, giggles, and a variety of musical notes can also accompany some "ahhhs."

"Open up, Rosie," I said. It was a house call and she was sitting near the window of her kitchen. "Now, open wide. Say ahhh."

At the very moment I placed the stick on her tongue, one of the cows that was grazing in the field just outside the window bellowed a very loud "Moo!"

The Country Doctor

I was so startled that I nearly lost the depressor down her throat.

"Rosie!" I teased. "Your voice sounds different. You've got a bad case of laryngitis."

Say hhhA, Rosie. Whoops. Let's try that again.
I had the tongue depressor in backward.

Interlude 5

More Quick Fixes

For a quick and inexpensive test of your lung capacity, try one of these simple and reasonably informative self-tests:

- Climb a flight of steps at a moderate pace without getting short of breath.
- Blow out a match with un-pursed lips.
- Hold your breath to a count of 30 seconds.

If you can't do any one of these, you may have a developing lung problem or you're pretty out of shape.

For those of you who are self-caring enough to do regular breast examinations for lumps, remember to do it in the tub or shower where soapy water or shaving cream makes palpation much more effective. This is especially important for women.

Chapter 6

On the Run

A big part of cure begins with the wish to be, then the want, then the will.

Bruno was a firm believer in not doing anything if it were not absolutely necessary. It was enough for him to be gainfully employed as a service station attendant. Beyond that, any other physical event was against his perception of predestination.

"Tell me, Doc, what can I do about my weight?" he occasionally asked when I stopped by for gas and oil and other Chunker needs. Bruno was five foot six inches tall and weighed 275 pounds. I wondered why he hadn't done something long before we had become acquainted.

"Bruno," I said. "We've talked before about watching your diet. Have you ever thought about exercise?"

"Oh, sure," he replied. "I've thought about it enough to decide not to do it. When I was born, God gave me only so many heartbeats for my life, and nothing I do will give me any more."

Alive and Well

With a medical IQ that low, I figured I didn't have much chance of convincing him otherwise, but over the ten years I knew him, I kept trying. On a number of occasions, I urged him to consider some form of fitness. I felt obliged to keep after him.

"You have high blood pressure, Bruno," I tried to reason with him. "There's a good chance you wouldn't have to take medicine if you lost weight. How about some type of sport? Do you hunt?"

"Why should I hunt? I didn't lose anything," he was quick to reply. So, his medical IQ ratcheted down a few more points, and I never did make any inroads on his attitude toward some form of exercise.

Bruno kept insisting that when he had used up his number of God-given heartbeats, it would be the end. I never knew just what he thought that number was, but I figured it was a lot less than it should have been when he died at age forty-five.

The likes of Bruno have been a frequent reminder to myself that fitness is important. The closer I came to middle-age, the more acute that idea became. Until then, my time and energy were spent in medical practice to the exclusion of taking care of my physical and emotional health. Fair, fat, and forty looked back at me from the mirror one day and, for the first time in years, I really looked back at myself and didn't think much of what I saw. At five feet four inches tall, 150 pounds was way too much for my small frame. The vision reminded me of how I felt, too--oldish, logy, and out of condition. My ego got into the act and screamed at my id with a loud and mocking laugh.

"That's enough!" I shouted back. "I'll do something about it and right quick."

Until then, my only physical activity outside of work was wild game hunting during the months of October through December. It was the season for stalking rabbits and grouse in fields thick with three-foot-tall goldenrod and aster. My two and a half foot legs would ache to the bone with the weariness of treading through an unforgiving obstacle course such as that.

The following year, I resolved to get into condition for the task before hunting season arrived. In April, as soon as the weather was suitable, I became reacquainted with an old love, cross-country running. At first, I lasted for a short quarter of a mile, then a half, then one. Distance gradually increased to five miles a day, five days a week, day or night, in all kinds of weather--sun and rain, hot and cold. By midwinter I could run 25 miles a day and felt ready for an official marathon. I decided to start with the top at Boston. I didn't plan to win, but I did plan to finish.

Alive and Well

As I reached the midpoint at Wellesley College, Billy Rogers was crossing the finish line in downtown Boston. Two and a half hours later, I, too, reached the end and announced to myself I had just won the race.

By the end of the second hunting season, I felt so much better--mentally, physically, and spiritually--that I could not stop running. I felt more physically fit in my fifties and sixties than I had in my twenties and thirties. My mental functions became clearer and sharper. As the "runner's high" kicked in, two miles into a run, creative ideas for my writing projects seemed to literally drop out of my subconscious into my conscious mind and into my writing arm. A spiritual dimension gradually came over me, completing a balanced wholeness with my physical and mental self. At my present three score and ten years of age, life is even more desirable, more necessary, and more pleasurable.

On the other hand, many of my friends and neighbors considered my running to be a strange, silly-looking thing, especially in thunder storms and snow squalls.

It became more than just fitness and fun. It was meditative for the heart and soul and a reacquaintance with nature. I enjoy being on country roads. I find myself running with porcupines and rabbits, raccoons and foxes, and other indigenous wildlife. It has been a childlike game over the years. I've avoided a rattlesnake now and then by high jumping an extra length with my stride.

A very large black bear, standing some eight feet tall and several hundred feet ahead, in the middle of the road, was more confused than I was scared. I continued running head-on. The runner's high had tranced me out and psyched the bear onto all fours as he rambled off into the woods. Too numb and dumb to be frightened at the time, the encounter came back to haunt me in nocturnal nightmares for several weeks.

Country roads are at their darkest on moonless, star-filled nights, and an unexpected brush with wildlife can be a sudden event. I remember an instance when the tree canopy of summer had converted my runway into a pitch-black tunnel, and suddenly, a well-antlered buck pranced out of the woods on my left. Just as we were about to collide, his instinct and mine prompted each of us to swerve away from the other, with his breath snorting into my face and my running shirt hanging on the tip of his antlers.

I was too startled to think for the next thirty feet. I clumsily crashed through a blockade meant to alert travelers to the washed-out bridge a few yards beyond. As I plunged into the cold water of North Creek, my breath was instantly restored, and I knew I had reached the turn around for that particular run.

Alive and Well

Long-distance runs on Mountain Country roads reacquaint me with nature, with the rhyme and reason of its rhythms and seasons. I bask in the joy of a heavy, summer rain storm, when the sky turns rapidly from blue to gray to black within a few blinks of an eye. Thunder and lightning assert themselves over my runway with mighty sound and flashing fury. It is the type of storm that usually comes in June after a dry spell of several weeks. The season's first hay crop has been cut and gathered together in rectangular bales, mushroom stalks, or rolls. What had been a neat field of virile green timothy before hay-making time now looks like a very bad haircut.

The storm is heralded by a sky full of wild, voluminous, steel-blue, dark-gray, and coal-black thunderheads. They appear suddenly and are followed by a dense cloud cover that obscures the heavens from horizon to horizon.

Over the distant hills and valleys, a wide vertical column of rain falls from beneath a large thunderhead. It seems like the plug has been yanked out of a colossal tub in which a very dirty giant has just taken his Saturday-night bath. It becomes a dense, wet wall moving rapidly in my direction.

The rain is so thick it turns broad daylight into the darkness of night and so heavy that raindrops fuse into sweeping sheets of water.

The Country Doctor

One bolt of lightning after another streaks through the sky in all directions, many at the same time. The long ones begin high and far away, at the apex of the sky, then streak downward as if a great handful of fingernails were etching their way across the back surface of a spherical mirror. Some bolts jump off one cloud to another or to the earth below. Others glow up from behind the horizon like spotlights for a spectacular stage show.

The zigzagging streaks of white-hot light are a wild wonder to behold as they sear through the dark skies. Trying to see it all is like watching a dozen tennis matches all at the same time or a sky full of rainbows.

The end of the storm is no less marvelous. The land and its flora and fauna is as divinely clean as a thoroughly scrubbed and rinsed newborn baby. Birds are quick to sing again, clearer and sweeter than before the rain. Wildflower purples, yellows, and reds are definitely brighter. Blade and leaf is so pungent it can be tasted as well as smelled. Everything sparkles and tingles with a new enthusiasm for living and growing.

"Why do you carry that stick when you're running?" my friend Tom asked.

"That's my anti-animal weapon."

"Whaddya mean by that?"

Alive and Well

"Whether I'm on city streets or country roads," I replied, "I meet one kind of animal or another. I've been running long distance for 25 years, and from the beginning, I've protected myself with this stick."

"I can't see how that would be much protection against a determined animal," Tom retorted, "tame or wild."

"Animals are territorial creatures," I continued, "dogs especially. When I run by someone's property, whether I'm on the sidewalk or a country road, dogs watch me come and go, barking the entire time I'm in sight.

"The greatest scare is when they're loose. That's when my stick comes into play. If the sight of my stick doesn't stop them in their tracks, I'll run toward them, waving it and yelling as loud as I can. I've never failed to route a dog in the opposite direction. I wouldn't be without this stick no matter where I'm running."

"Doesn't it interfere?" Tom asked. "Seems to me it would be a handicap when you're in training. Doesn't it curb the swing of your arms, cut down on your time?"

"Yes, it does a little," I admitted. "But, remember what I've told you before. I don't run to make time. I don't run to win. I run to endure. All I want at the end of a race is to finish. I want to be standing on my own two feet."

"Have you ever won a race?" Tom continued.

The Country Doctor

"Sure I have, but no more than a half dozen or so. That's not the reason I run. For me, races are for fun. There is a special feeling connected with running in a crowd, an extra incentive. The best running for me, though, is when I do my daily five miles alone, all by myself."

"Well, it sounds strange to me that you don't run to win," Tom frowned. "Why bother?"

"After I ran my first three marathons at the age of forty-five, I decided that the three top runners in any 26.2 mile run were: the first man, the first woman, and the one who finishes last."

"Last?" questioned Tom.

"Darn right," I confirmed. "After all, that person ran for the longest time! All three of them should have equal billing.

"Some twenty years ago, the last person to finish in the New York City Marathon after seven and a half hours, had a prosthetic leg from his hip down. In my book, he was the top winner!

"When I, myself, was 65 and in the over-fifty category, I was competing with runners fifteen years younger than I. That's when I decided marathons are an overrated media event, not an athletic effort that recognizes the many silent heroines and heros.

Alive and Well

"And I like running on country roads the best, especially when I'm in the mountains. Nowhere else can you experience such wonderful sights and sounds. The joy is so much greater, and my anti-animal stick is just as necessary."

I learned a good lesson about wild animals when I was country doctoring in Ethiopia. I had noticed that the natives, when they were out in open country and on mountain roads, always carried a stick with them. It was about six feet long, and they carried it across the back of their shoulders with both arms dangling over it.

"Nagub," I asked one day after we had become well acquainted, "why do the local people carry a stick with them?"

"Listen," he said, cupping his hand to his ear. "Do you hear that noise?"

"It sounds something like a dog, halfway between a bark and a laugh," I answered.

"It's a laughing hyena," Nagub related. "It can be vicious and dangerous. It's not unusual for them to attack people in the open country. When there's a pack of them, they can be very aggressive."

"Okay, I'll take one of those sticks, now! But, what do you do if the animal is a lion or tiger or some other such creature?" I asked.

The Country Doctor

"I'll tell you what sometimes works. You yell as loud as you can. My father always said you can scare any animal off by yelling at the top of your voice. It works if you can yell louder than a lion can roar or a tiger can growl."

Well, that was one experience I could do without, but I still always carry my stick. It worked in Africa and it works in my own backyard. I've never been without it since.

Jogging is healthy for the feet and legs;
it's good for the ground too--it makes it feel needed.

Interlude 6

Common Sense and Fitness
Some Highlights

1. Common sense and fitness are essential to your physical, mental, and spiritual health.

2. Anyone can do something whether sitting, standing, walking, confined to a wheelchair, or bedfast.

3. Cardiovascular exercise benefits your heart, lungs, and circulation.

4. Musculoskeletal exercise is good for your muscles, tendons, bones, and joints.

5. Types of exercise:

    a. Action (for cardiovascular function)
    b. Endurance (to last)
    c. Isometric (for muscle mass)
    d. Stretching (for flexibility)
    e. Toning (for smooth movement)
    f. Conditioning (for strength)
    g. Strengthening (for power)

6. In addition to whatever you do at your job, engage in some form of exercise three to five times weekly for at least a half hour.

7. Pick the time of day in keeping with your convenience and biorhythm.

Chapter 7

Sugar and Spice

A miracle drug is one that does what it says on the label.

Just out of internship and with a little specialty training under my stethoscope, I was practicing inside the walls of a steel mill. It was my first stint at full-fledged medical practice after graduating from the University of Pittsburgh, where I had spent three years specializing in industrial and environmental medicine.

The dispensary was within one hundred yards of the blast furnace, and I was in the front line of industrial medicine. Injured workers did not go to the hospital Emergency Room two miles away. They came to me first. They were rugged, hard-working men who made iron and steel for the automobile industry. It was not unusual to have someone saunter into the dispensary with a stub on one hand and the amputated finger in the other.

"Fix it for me, Doc," they would announce. "Put it together so I can get back to work."

My Old-World patients in the mills of iron and steel were very emphatic when it came to their medical theories. They advised me, in no uncertain terms, how they protected themselves against viruses during the cold season of the year.

"I take one pink aspirin every day before I go to bed," Mike said. "I start in September and take it 'til springtime. Haven't had a cold and haven't missed work in thirty years."

And that was my introduction to psychology and placebos and the smoldering idea that, sometimes, some people just might know what's best for them. It was difficult for me to argue with Mike's kind of success or his conviction.

Aspirin tablets were generic then. They were given out to the ship's company in the Navy, when I was a bell-bottomed sailor, and to workers in the dispensaries of steel mills, coal mines, and railroads. Some were white and some were pink. A man could have his choice.

I sometimes wondered if the tablets worked because they were free or because of their color. But, there was one thing I had accepted. For those rugged men of steel, the tablets had to be pink.

I didn't need to look at my schedule to know who was next on the appointment book. I could tell by the end of my nose. It was wild leek time in the Allegheny Mountains, and for a few weeks in early spring Hank kept his body and his home and his surroundings, everywhere,

The Country Doctor

engulfed in an intense aroma of wild leeks. The smell was amazingly pungent. I expected to actually see its vapors following him around like his very own little white cloud.

I wondered why he ever came to the office to see me, for he gave so much credit to the medicinal value of leeks. He never had a complaint. Nothing was ever physically amiss. He wanted no treatment from me. After awhile, I decided he visited me just to be reassured that his leeks were working and that he could take care of himself.

Now, when it comes to herbs, how can the average all-American resist poetic names such as leek and garlic and onion, along with such musical names as:

Good Earth Chaparral that purifies the blood but can also cause hepatitis.
Chlorophyll Comfrey which promotes healthy skin but can also cause liver and kidney problems.
Ephedra or *Ma Huang* which is supposed to suppress the appetite, although it can also elevate blood pressure.
Lobelia or *Indian tobacco*, an energizer that can also overwork the heart.
Yohimbe which counteracts impotence but can also cause weakness, fatigue, and paralysis.

Alive and Well

Labels on such poetically-named products announce their benefits while discretely omitting the side effects. Adverse effects are a possibility when unregulated herbal supplements, over-the-counter, or health food store products are used. Allergic reactions are also a threat. It's a more risky form of treatment when compared to using generic or prescription medicines which are regulated by government agencies.

On the other hand, there are some herbs with equally musical names that, even if they don't help, won't hurt if mixed with equal parts of common sense:

Camomile tea relaxes the muscles of the bowel to relieve indigestion.

Echinacea may increase your resistance to upper respiratory infections.

Feverfew leaves may help migraine headaches if you can avoid ulcers of the mouth and tongue.

Ginger is helpful for nausea and motion sickness.

Hawthorne extract dilates blood vessels for relieving angina and lowering blood pressure.

Valerian extract can help with insomnia and nervousness if your nose will tolerate the odor of musty, sharp cheese and dirty, wet socks.

It is interesting to note that in the United States, herbs and over-the-counter drugs are used to the tune of billions of dollars a year--in large part because we like to help ourselves, return to nature, or bypass the professional health care provider for reasons of convenience, cost, or bad experiences.

While doing so, it is good to call on common sense, that most uncommon of all senses, and to keep in mind that promoting and selling herbs is a business. That means advertising, and that means profits.

Surely, there is cause to wonder about a product label which promotes such diverse promises as "Guaranteed to help you lose weight if you're fat and gain weight if you're thin," or "Lower your sugar if it's too high and raise it if it's too low."

The labels I enjoy most are those that credit a single product for treating insomnia, jet lag, impotence, fatigue, nervousness, cancer, headaches, fractured eyelashes, and dislocated hangnails--all in one dose.

The eyebrow of caution should rise, as well, at the vague, general claims of "strengthen the heart," "enhance sex life," "slow the aging process," and "boost the energy level."

"Now, tell me how you're doing, Millie," I asked. "Tell me how you take it." I was curious to know why she was so confident about the results.

"Well, I started out with nine yellow raisins soaked overnight in a teaspoonful of brandy," she related. "Have to be fresh soaked so they don't spoil. It's an old Indian remedy. Learned about it from my mother's cousin who was five percent pure Seneca blood."

"So how's it working for you?" I questioned once again, in need of more information to make up my own mind about still another home remedy.

"It's working good. Better than anything you've prescribed for me. A lot less expensive, too."

"Are you still taking it the same? Every day? Once a day in the morning?"

"Yep. I take a large tablespoon now," Millie rambled on. "You know I have a touch of this shaking palsy and I've been losing some from the teaspoon.

"And, I take it four times a day. One dose was doing good but not lasting long enough. It's like a lot of the medicine you've prescribed for me--every four hours works just right. I'm down to three raisins a dose now, too. The spoon's less crowded and I spill less that way."

The Country Doctor

"Well, I can't argue with your success or with your satisfaction, Millie." I wasn't about to tell her that it was more likely that the brandy and not the raisin mix that was treating her. Besides, she wasn't hurting herself.

Personally, I have believed in home remedies ever since Grandfather spit tobacco juice in my ear to cure my annual swimmer's itch. It burned so much and smelled so bad, one treatment always worked. I guaranteed it.

Like many small towns in Pennsylvania mountain country, ours had a little old lady with a pointed hat, and a lumpy nose to match, who removed warts from a host of fingers when I was a growin' up boy. A quick rub for a penny a wart did the trick. Sometimes, there were a dozen or more per head (on the hands). The pennies disappeared even quicker than the warts into a deep apron pocket. The warts were soon forgotten by the children, and the pennies were well-remembered by the little old lady on her way to the bank. It was a pretty good moonlight job back then.

A fingernail infection was cured with wagon-wheel axle grease which was upgraded to coal-black ichthammol ointment later on. My body wanted to get rid of the infection, and the infection wanted to get out from under the smell of that odorous, black stuff so badly, a cure was miraculously quick.

Alive and Well

Medicinal herbs were a big part of the scene back then. Some had migrated from Europe, others were recommended by Native Americans, and still others had been conjured up by the frontier farmers of early America. Even today, herbs are the source of about half of our more refined prescriptions and over-the-counter products.

Of course, who among us can forget Vapo-Rub®--the stronger the better--especially when used with a Turkish towel over the head and around the neck of the victim, buried under a woolen blanket in a dark corner of the house, far away from the rest of the family.

And there was the chest poultice, made with a horseradish base. The more it bit, the more it burned, the better it worked.

On the other hand, common sense should tell you that a tumor on the skin can easily be cut out and thrown away by a surgeon. The procedure is quicker and less expensive than any mega stuff taken into your stomach or rubbed onto your skin.

When chest pain is caused by a blocked coronary artery, the cardiologist is the best bet for reaming it out or bypassing it rather than relying on multi doses of garlic. 'Tis better to open an artery with angioplasty than the nose with garlic!

The Country Doctor

Yet, it can be the case that a preventive common sense amount of garlic in the diet can help the lipids to pass more readily through the arteries.

Alternative medicine, the various ways and means of treating human suffering outside the conventional medical profession, has come a long way. It now covers a wide spectrum of ills--physical, mental, and spiritual--and an equally broad array of means, all the way from blinking lights, primal scream, acutouch, acupressure, acupuncture, meditation, herbs, sound, music, dance, aromas, etc., etc., etc. Now that the idea has caught on, the cost has become pretty competitive.

Use of these ways and means requires as much common sense as prescription and over-the-counter medications. All have their share of toxic and placebo, as well as beneficial, effects.

Since they are rapidly catching up with regular medical care, caution is the watchword, no matter your choice of regular, alternative, or self-help home remedies and herbs.

Herbs, for example, have the possible disadvantage of poor quality control and precision. They may be diluted by any number of inactive components. You can take a lot and pay a lot to get a small part of the proper dose.

And yet, prescription drugs are so controlled and precise, it can be all too easy to get a toxic amount.

Alive and Well

Adverse effects are rampant, be they by prescription, over-the-counter, or health food store products.

Remember, all forms of medical care have their share of side effects whether it be a technique, a service, or a product. When providers push their wares too hard on you and your ills, beware of monetary motivation. Some practice a service for a fee. Others sell a product for money.

He who borrows spices from others is living on borrowed thyme.

Interlude 7

Symptoms and Signs

If you would like to be a better-informed patient, it is helpful to know the difference between a symptom and a sign.

A symptom lets you know something is amiss with your physical or mental health. It's what you feel; it's your complaint.

A sign is something that can be seen or heard by yourself or the doctor or someone else.

Sore throat is a symptom; a red throat is a sign of strep throat.

A cough is a symptom; congestion detected by stethoscope is a sign of pneumonia.

Between you and your symptoms and your caregiver's signs, the two of you can make the best sense of what's wrong and what to do about it.

Alive and Well

Chapter 8

Ol' Scrooge

Power and money can be as poisonous in medical care as in other fields of human endeavor.

When the door to my examining room flew open unpreceded by a courtesy knock, I didn't need to look up to know it was the hospital director. Ol' Scrooge couldn't have cared less whether I might have been in the middle of examining a patient. Pushing a letter into my face and demanding that I read it immediately, he was his usual, unsavory, doomsday self.

I already knew the contents of the letter, so I didn't bother to take it from his hand. The hospital underground had alerted me two days earlier by way of Scrooge's personal secretary. In my five years of practice in "his" hospital, I had never known him to be the bearer of good tidings, for me or for anyone else.

Health care is big industry these days in this confounded, complex, contemporary world. Hospitals and clinics alike are run like businesses. It's no wonder that the number of people who administrate medical care exceeds that of income-generating providers--physicians, nurses, technicians, and the like. There is a great

The Country Doctor

hierarchy of executives now: CEOs, CFOs, vice presidents of this and that, and support staffs of vertiginous proportions. What a dramatic contrast to my earlier days in small hospitals across the country.

"It's from the executive committee," Scrooge blurted out. "You are to read it right away and in my presence."

Casually, I opened it and quickly browsed the message to read, "You are no longer permitted to work in the Emergency Room without supervision by the surgical staff."

Like the lifetime that can occasionally flash through one's mind, my years of association with that place and its staff spun before me like my first helicopter stall out.

In the beginning, I was a welcomed colleague in the 50-bed hospital with its handful of staff. Because many of my patients had followed me from my office 25 miles away, in Greenville, the hospital staff viewed me as an additional source of referrals for the specialists and the other hospital services. After three years of success, a witch hunt of my hospital patient records had been initiated by two other medical staff members. The executive committee claimed the result justified their threat to limit my practice privileges and call me on the carpet for alleged poor-quality care and unprofessional conduct.

Scrooge's implosion, although expected, left me baffled and thoroughly agitated. I muddled the attack through my mind and heart. I could see no reason for it. I got along well with all support people in the hospital from the kitchen, housekeeping, and maintenance personnel to the nurses, secretaries, and technicians. My patient load had steadily increased, and I knew I was contributing significantly to the hospital's business. I asked myself what motive they could possible have, but none came to mind at that moment.

"Give me the rest of the week to think this over," I remarked, reaching for the door and ushering him out of the office.

As he made his brisk exit, I watched him disappear down the long corridor.

Reflecting on his obnoxious behavior, I had difficulty envisioning that man as the administrator of a caregiving institution. Were it not so tragic, it might have been some scene from a slapstick comedy come to life.

In those days, little community hospitals were managed by either a director of nursing, who evolved into the position as a semi-retired supervisor; a business office manager, untrained and inexperienced as an administrator; or a well-beyond-retirement, disabled physician, equally without management and business acumen. Scrooge was a former office manager and, symbolic of his day, ill equipped to play the part of top administrator for a health care institution.

The other members of that archaic, hospital-control team were two doctors, Hugo and Rodriguez. They had been at the hospital long enough to believe they personally owned it by virtue of adverse possession. Providing quality care had no place on their agenda. Territorial imperative was their number one priority.

I am convinced it never occurred to Hugo to stop, look, and listen to what was going on inside himself that might relate to what was going on around him. He simply did not know what was going on. He had an underdeveloped internal mechanism for compassion and caring.

When it came to looking for cause and effect, his focus was always external. If something were not going smoothly, it was Hugo's nature to place blame with something or somebody other than himself. On the other hand, he gave himself plenty of credit when things went right.

His entire life, professional and personal, was spent working his fool head off in his quest to satisfy a deep insecurity. The pseudo-reassurance of things material--a busy practice, a nice home, three cars, and the reputation of being "oh so busy"--was his agenda. He was, indeed, the epitome of a certain brand of contemporary doctor.

Rodriguez, on the other hand, was very aware of his surroundings. He was adept at making things happen to his own best advantage and to the painful disadvantage of everyone else. He lacked the moral and ethical fiber to do otherwise, as though he had been possessed by an amoral psychosocial mentality.

Those two egomaniacs took every opportunity possible to confront each other, always with the same explosive results--two irresistible forces and two immovable objects. It was a professional tragedy in an institution of healing, but they were typical examples of a class of health care providers branded by the experience of early childhood insecurities, driven by fear for their emotional lives. Their chronic apprehension was so strong that it prevented them from looking at and helping themselves. Instead, it was easier to look at others, to "help" others. Their need was to be reassured by pseudo-omnipotence and all the material possessions of their trade. It didn't seem to matter that they "worked themselves to death" in the process.

Those unsavory ingredients of hospital operations in the "dark-age" days of early twentieth-century medical care were cemented together by the odorous glue of a community board that served as the catalyst for the group's inbred mentality. They were incapable of seeing over the edge of the ruts they were stuck in.

It was no surprise that ol' Scrooge could not wait until Friday for my answer. He returned on Thursday without invitation. Bursting into the examining room, he shoved another letter into my face. Again, he demanded that I read it immediately. To rid myself of him as quickly as possible, I read, "The executive committee has, hereby, revoked your hospital privileges. Effective this date you

The Country Doctor

are no longer a member of the staff. You can no longer practice in this hospital."

Still not surprised, I was none-the-less provoked at the lack of intestinal fortitude on the part of the medical staff to meet with me face to face. To confront me by way of that unprofessional hound dog prompted me to say, "I will be dropping by my attorney's office when I leave. Let your cronies know I will be suing the lot of you unless this decision is quickly revoked." I turned and walked away leaving the letter behind me in the wastebasket.

Over the following months, through conversations with the hospital underground, my patients, and my attorney, the scenario became quite clear to me. I had been doing too well while Hugo and Rodriguez, due to their personal insecurities, believed their "business" to be melting away. I found out, also, that the alleged reason for the dismissal was that I had continued to use black, silk, suture material for repairing wounds in the Emergency Room after the rest of the medical staff had switched to a new "plastic" kind. The stiffness of that rigid, fishing-tackle-type stitching never appealed to me. It was too likely to tear through the repaired skin. I had been satisfied with my time-proven technique. It had good healing results and as good, or better, a record for less wound infection than the plastic employed by the rest of the staff.

After two years of banter and battle with attorneys, plus the enormous support of many people, I was

Alive and Well

informed that the court had voided my hospital termination. Disappointed and disgusted with the hospital staff, but happy enough to be "officially reinstated," I left that professionally forsaken scene and looked forward to a brighter workplace.

Patient notes:

Thank you so much for the six-page letter you sent me explaining the hard situation you've had to face. I read every page four times. Never heard any ill rumors. You were a good doctor when I worked 3-11 shift at the hospital. The other doctors are jealous when a doctor is well liked by patients.

It was a great shock to receive your letter yesterday. I feel like someone grabbed my "security blanket" from me. Who will listen or care?

Sorry to hear that the bureaucracy got to you! <u>Sometime, somewhere,</u> you're going to have to make the other fellow leave!!!

The passing away of the likes of that scene was the eventual demise of an epoch in community hospital care

The Country Doctor

that had to happen. Many were doomed to extinction. Others converted to convalescent, nursing, and residential homes. Others were swallowed up as a part of large managed care organizations.

Ol' Scrooge was the last of an abominable health care team--a hanger-on beyond his time, perpetuated, in part, by the psycho-social pathology of professional staffs, administrators, boards of directors, and unenlightened community "leaders."

There are definitely some things about those "good ol' days" that are best left to the past--dead and gone.

Time wounds all heels.

Interlude 8

Headache

Headache is one of the most common complaints experienced by human beings. Daily, some forty million people in the United States suffer from the affliction that is responsible for more disability than heart disease, stroke, and cancer combined.

Headaches are disruptive, both for work and daily living. And, according to medical records from the Garden of Eden, they frequently serve as a contraceptive.

Only about five percent of all headaches are caused by serious underlying disease such as brain tumor, aneurysm, or stroke. The greatest number, ninety-five percent, are tension headaches brought on by physical or emotional stress.

The migraine type is relatively uncommon, accounting for less than five percent. Many people claim to have this type on the basis of curbstone consultations with family, friends, and neighbors. More often than not, it is not the case.

Victims of headaches that recur over a period of time owe it to themselves, family, friends, and employer to have a medical evaluation. A diagnosis should be established as to the cause and careful professional evaluation is needed for the best possible management.

The Country Doctor

Chapter 9

What! A Helicopter

It's a great satisfaction to do what people say can't be done.

"What do you mean you bought a helicopter?!" shouted Sam, my accountant. "You don't even know how to fly one!"

"I'll learn to fly it, as soon as it's on the landing pad behind the office," I replied.

"You're going to spend $65,000 on a gamble like that? Suppose you can't do it?" he bellowed, a little louder that time.

"Oh, I know I can do it," I said. "Besides I'm only going to lease the copter. It would be too costly to buy it outright. Give me six months and I'll have my wings. In the meantime, I'm betting on myself. The risk will give me one heck of a good reason not to fail. And, you can be my first passenger."

"You're a country doctor," my staunch, ol' accountant hollered. "Remember?"

"I do, Sam. I'm reminded of it every day as I look at my patient schedule. And I feel it, too, at the end of the day."

Alive and Well

"Why don't you get a horse and buggy?" he said, throwing up his hands as he continued his discouraging words.

"Now, Sam, you know very well that things are not what they used to be. No matter how much you and I and a lot of others wish for it, its never going to be that way again. The most I can do, the most I want to do, is to practice medicine with a country-doctor attitude, be that in the office or in the home or on the farm. It matters not whether I walk, drive my Chunker, or fly a helicopter.

"Just like people anywhere, the country folks want and need medical care that is reasonably accessible. It doesn't matter to them whether I arrive by horse, wheels, or wings.

"I'm not going to lie to you, Sam. If I had my druthers I'd just as soon spend my entire day, from daybreak to dark, riding a buggy all over the countryside. But, that wouldn't get the job done, and you know why," I continued. "For the past three years, my office has been getting more and more crowded. People are traveling from all directions as far as forty miles one way.

"There's no point in having a bigger office. There's no place to expand; and even if there were, I couldn't get enough help to see everyone. Besides, I don't want those folks traveling that distance in all kinds of weather, especially in the wintertime.

"I've thought of a solution, I know of a better way. I have an idea, a good idea!" I informed him, excited to be telling someone about it. "And, I just have to do this!"

"Okay, let's hear it," Sam relented, hunkering down in his chair and half covering his ears in dejected resignation. "I'm not at all sure I want to hear this, but I'll listen," he added in a mumble.

I smiled, noting his ears. His curiosity would not allow him to cover them completely.

"These are the 1960's," I began. "You know as well as I that family doctors are fast becoming a shadow of the past. Every few months or so, another general practitioner leaves or retires or dies. Why, in this part of Pennsylvania, with the medical center growing by leaps and bounds, we have more new surgeons and neurologists than we do family doctors. I don't see that changing in the foreseeable future."

"I'm waiting to hear your plan," Sam sighed, shoulders and knees drawn in, eyes partially closed. He appeared so tensed in his seated posture as though in severe pain.

"I've been wanting to talk to you about it," I replied. "I've been tossing it around in my mind for quite a while.

"Look at Cedarville, a community of about 500 residents. They have a decent, small office, quite new, where, for the past ten years, doctors have come and gone

Alive and Well

every few months. The town's people are eager for a practitioner to take over the building and become a permanent fixture. They need an ongoing, dependable doctor. Yet, there is no physician available to them within twenty-five miles of that place.

"Do you realize what that means? Some of them are traveling forty miles to my valley office. Others go to the medical center in Linden City. But, most of them go nowhere. They simply refuse to travel that kind of distance, and, in the meantime, all kinds of medical problems go unattended--acute illnesses such as sore throats, chest pains, and coughs. And so do the complications of rheumatic fever, heart disease, and pneumonia! Things like diabetes and high blood pressure come on and advance into serious, often fatal, complications without ever being diagnosed.

"Then there's Seneca, twenty miles north of here. Except for the fact that it's closer, that village is no different from Cedarville. And, there's Penn's Lake to the west. It's in the same predicament. I'm talking about rural areas, Sam. Although it's true that Linden City and the medical center is only fifteen miles away, that doesn't mean much to country folks of the kind we both know.

"A helicopter could take me to satellite offices in those locations in a quarter of the time it would take to drive the distance. Just think of the time and inconvenience we could save those people.

"We could staff the offices with some of the physician's assistants that are coming out of the new training schools for medics. Those people are very capable. They have had experience as medical corpsmen in the Viet Nam fiasco, in addition to formal training.

"Family doctors are disappearing way too quickly in these rural areas and no one seems to care! No one is replacing them!! With three satellite offices and the main office, just think of how many more people could be cared for!!!

"Sure as I can drive wheels, I know I can wing a helicopter. What do you say?" I asked, catching my breath.

"I hope you know what you're getting into," Sam replied.

"That's the point; I don't. But that's the fun of it! Isn't life exciting?"

"Humph, I'm not even going to think about it."

He stood up, stretched, and headed toward the door. "I am just going to crunch numbers and count dollars."

A confident pilot has both feet planted firmly in midair.

Interlude 9

Phobia

A phobia is an exaggerated or illogical fear of something. For example, aerophobia is a fear of air.

My latest review of phobias came up with a list of two hundred ten ranging all the way from A to Z, acrophobia (a fear of heights) to zoophobia (a fear of animals). There is even one called phophobia which is the fear of fearing.

Phobias can be mild, such as avoiding ladders and black cats. Other phobias can severely limit the victim's activities of daily living.

Learning more about your own particular phobia is the first step in doing something about it. When sufficiently severe, your professional caregiver can guide you through the steps to help yourself. It is possible to desensitize yourself by being exposed to the fear little bits at a time. It works for allergies and it can work for phobias.

Chapter 10

Curbstone Experts

Be careful your medicine doesn't beat your disease and you to death at the same time.

"You've got the hives, Nannie," I said, the instant I looked at the swellings of various sizes and shapes all over her body. "You're allergic to something. What is it?"

"Well, I don't know," she replied. "Can't think of anything. I'm so uncomfortable. It's terrible itchy. I feel weak. I'm getting short of breath, having trouble swallowing."

"Whatever it is, you need something fast! A shot of adrenalin will quickly get you over the worst. I'll also give you some prednisone to be sure it will go away completely over the next few hours.

"In the meantime, what have you gotten into? Anything you've eaten? Have you taken any medicine of any kind? Are you sick in any way?"

"Well, I came down with a cold three days ago when I was visiting my sister in Akron," Nannie replied. "She gave me something she took herself a few weeks before, an antibiotic. Tetracycline she called it."

Alive and Well

"Nannie!" I exclaimed. "Don't you remember? You reacted to Terramycin® five years ago when I treated you for a case of bronchitis. It's the same kind of thing. I told you never to take that type of mycin again."

"Well, I do recollect now. And after this, I reckon I'll never forget again."

"What can I do for you, Richie?" I asked as he staggered into the treatment room to collapse in a chair. "What's up with you?"

He answered me with a spasm of coughing that sounded like it was coming from his feet. He coughed so hard, I thought he was about to fall apart like one of his dilapidated old cars.

"How long have you had that cough? You look pretty awful."

"Three weeks now," he replied.

"Well, tell me more about it. Have you had that kind of cough for that long? What have you been doing about it?"

"Uhh, it just started out as a head cold. Then a sore throat. I've had the cough for two weeks now."

"Have you taken anything--Tylenol®, cold medicine, cough syrup?"

"Yes, I've been taking these." He pulled a handful of blue and white capsules out of his pocket along with some loose coins, some throat lozenges, and some white tablets that looked like aspirin. I recognized the capsules as ampicillin.

"Where did you get these capsules?" I demanded. "Do you know what they are?"

"Well, no, I don't know. I got them from my sister-in-law. She had a chest cold a month ago and they cured her after three weeks. She insisted my cough sounded just like hers. Knew they would work for me just like they did for her."

"Well, what did she have?" I asked. "How did she know you had the same thing? How do you know? And why are you in here to see me?"

"Can't you see? I'm sick. All over. I can hardly stand. My appetite has been shot for a week now. You've got to do something and stop asking all those fool questions."

"Oh, I'll do something, Richie," I said, "after I tell you how foolish it was to have taken someone else's medication when you should have known better.

"You're smarter than that about motors and clutches and brakes, but when it comes to taking care of your health, your medical IQ seems to be about as low as your energy level at the moment. Don't you realize what a chance you took? You would have been better off with nothing. Of all the kinds of medicine available, someone else's is the worst. If you're not going to consult with a doctor, I'd rather see you use your grandmother's home remedies."

As a doctor, I find it interesting and sobering that the American public consumes billions of doses of medicine by pill, liquid, and capsule every year to the tune of billions of dollars. It can be as equally baffling to imagine where all that medicine comes from, beyond the physician-prescribed brand-name and generic varieties. Unfortunately, there is an abundance of illegal and black-market drugs which contribute to the consumption.

Brand-name and generic medications depend on a diagnosis of your illness by the doctor. They are likely to be more accurate, reliable, and effective than the others.

Generics are a copy of the original and are known by their chemical rather than their proprietary names: diazepam for Valium®; digoxin for Lanoxin®; penicillin for Pen-Vee K®; and acetaminophen for Tylenol®. The difference in the spelling gives one an idea as to why doctors tend to prefer brand names to generics; they are easier to remember and quicker to write. The practice is also more beneficial to the brand-name manufacturer who is in the profit-making business.

The advantage of generic drugs is economy. They sell for thirty to eighty percent less than their brand-name counterparts. Since the initial cost of research and development of the drug was funded by a brand-name company, the manufacturers of the generic drugs need not incur that expense. Thus, a portion of the savings is passed on to the consumer.

The generic trade is also a very big one. At present, it is estimated to be a seven-billion-dollar-a-year business, currently manufacturing and selling some eight thousand products, all with Food and Drug Administration approval.

Despite the fact that a generic drug is supposed to be exactly the same as the brand name and absorbed from the stomach and intestine into the bloodstream at the same rate, generic drugs may not always be as therapeutically effective or as well tolerated as the brand name drugs.

Also available, are over-the-counter (OTC) medicines, those you get without a prescription. They can be purchased off the shelf of a drug or grocery store, a hardware store or gas station, a variety of convenience stores, or even, through the mail. They may be generic--that is a copy of the original brand name--such as ibuprofen for Advil®; or they may be the brand name itself--Advil® for ibuprofen.

Over-the-counter products are part of a multi-billion-dollar-a-year business that is rapidly growing. An increasing number of people are treating their own medical problems. And, the magnitude of the OTC medicine business is expected to become even greater as the public becomes more (and not necessarily better) informed in self diagnosis and self treatment.

Overuse and abuse increases right along with this popular trend. Since OTC medicine usage is powered by manufacturers' advertising and driven by profit, it is especially important to use a large dose of common sense to protect your health while, also, protecting your pocketbook. For example, aspirin and ibuprofen may cause serious side effects that are worse than the condition they are meant to treat. Adverse effects on the stomach, liver, and kidneys can be significant, especially in chronic and elderly users. At the same time, there are usually few warnings on the labels of these readily obtainable products.

In the case of prescription medications, the doctor and druggist are in control of what is used. With OTC medicines, only you and common sense are in control of what you use and whether it helps or hinders.

A common example of abuse of OTC medicines is the overuse of laxatives which, by itself, has developed into a major problem. The estimate of users range from five to ten percent of the U.S. population. That amounts to around twenty million people, most of whom are women or older adults. Abuse means that something, that really does no good, is being consumed and may be covering up an underlying, serious problem. In the case of laxatives, side effects of abuse include cramps, gas, diarrhea, nausea, vomiting, fluid and mineral loss, and a worsening of the constipation that they were meant to help.

It is certainly advisable to take a big dose of common sense along with each dose of OTC medicine.

How often have you taken a medication given to you by someone who decided you had the same condition as they?

There are those who will freely offer you their personal medication for a symptom that could be an indication of any one of numerous, different inflictions. People who engage in this type of sharing are referred to as "curbstone experts" and are as dangerous to your health as the disease itself. A curbstone expert is a friend, acquaintance, or relative who diagnoses your ailment by comparing your symptoms with their own or with the symptoms of someone they have known or heard or read about. They then proceed to treat you with their own medicine.

A cough, you know, can be of many different kinds and can be caused by nerves, allergy, infection, dust, vapors, smoke, or cancer.

Alive and Well

Be wary of the advice given by curbstone experts. Not only may their medications not rid you of your symptom, they may be detrimental to your health. If they do work, it may be due to random luck or the fact that you didn't need them in the first place.

Your best bet with curbstone medicines is not to take them. Instead, bring them to your doctor and ask for his or her advice. Just as often as not, your doctor will agree that the medication is safe for you and will provide you with a prescription. Don't take a chance on them otherwise.

Another serious threat to your health can be leftovers. They are the medicine bottles in the back of the medicine cabinet in the bathroom and behind the spice rack in the kitchen. The tool box, glove compartment, suitcase, and tackle box often contains outdated pills and capsules. Get rid of them! If they have not deteriorated into a toxic chemical, they aren't likely to be effective all those years after the date on the label has faded into illegibility.

The safest of all cures just might be Granny's meds or home remedies. They have been passed down from one generation to the next and, often, go all the way back to pioneer days. Some of these remedies came to the United States on the Mayflower. Others originated along with the

The Country Doctor

beginning of modern man, back there five thousand years or so ago. Still others came to us from our Native American ancestors.

Like medicines from other sources, Granny meds are of a wide assortment and vary all the way from the copper penny for warts and the copper bracelet for arthritis to snake oil for earaches. They may be anything from soup to nuts and sometimes are pretty nutsy.

No less than two generations ago, home cures in many families were commonly found in the pantry along with herbs for seasoning, flavoring, and fragrance.

Turpentine was one of Grandma's basic ingredients. It found its way into eardrops, cough syrup, and poultices. Onions and garlic were common ingredients in dozens of home remedies and have been scientifically proven to lower cholesterol and high blood pressure. Catnip is a nice ingredient in sedative teas for colicky babies and sleepless adults. In addition, chewing catnip leaves can reduce the pain of a toothache. It's "kitty approved," you know.

How well do granny medicines work when compared to other medications? Some claim there is no scientific proof that any of them work. While it is true that proof may not exist in the form of scientifically-controlled studies, it may be a significant fact that many of the world's medicines of today originated from herbal plants.

Also, proof may be in the fact that, for thousands of years, granny medicines have worked for billions of pioneers, Native Americans, Chinese, and people the world over. In my opinion, such proof may be as valid as any scientific study that is occasionally announced in newspapers and magazines where one headline might state, "Aspirin Is a Clear-cut Help to the Heart," and another study might conclude that "Aspirin Users Could Be Prone to Heart Disease."

The bottom line may be that granny meds work--and they won't hurt you if they don't--because both Granny and the patient believe they will. Is that any different than the confidence we place in a medication that comes from a visit to the doctor or one that has a high price tag? Some believe that "the more it costs, the better it works" or, for those that taste awful, "the worse the taste, the better the results." Others believe in freebies given to them by a friend or a product they choose off the shelf. In the final analysis, a placebo is a placebo regardless of its source.

Over-the-counter medicines are miracle drugs; a year's supply can disappear in a month.

Interlude 10

Still More Quick Fixes

A tad of castor oil, meat tenderizer, or ice cube massage are three quick fixes for itching insect bites, that is, if you're carrying such items in your pocket when you are out there amongst the insects.

Keep in mind that biting insects--mosquitos, gnats, flies--are discouraged by the liberal use of a repellant. But, don't depend on it for stinging insects--honey bees, wasps, hornets, yellow jackets. Your best defense for those is tight-fitting clothes and netting.

If you experience cracks in the skin of your fingers after frequent washings, especially in the wintertime, you will find it effective to cover them with tape, day and night, for two to three days. This method of treatment lessens the pain and encourages faster healing. To my mind, paper adhesive best conforms and clings to the fingers, and, a little bit goes a long way.

Chapter 11

Blackfoot Country

Can collective praise mitigate individual guilt?

So this is what it's like, I thought as my plane circled over a small village surrounded by a flat, treeless terrain. As far as I could see from two thousand feet in the air, it looked like an African desert. This is definitely different from my boyhood vision of an Indian reservation. Where are all those colorful teepees in that grassy meadow at the edge of a quiet lake? Where is the forest primeval?

I shook my head to rid my mind of the mountainous, hardwood forests of Northcentral Pennsylvania and assimilate the grassless plains that stretched to the horizon in every direction. Only the Rocky Mountains in the west, some twenty miles away, interrupted what reminded me of the surface of a gently rolling South Pacific sea.

I could understand why the local license plate logo identified the state of Montana as "Big Sky Country." The broad expanse of land allowed for a sky to match. I had never seen such magnificent rainbows nor so many at one time. The end of those celestial promises stretched from

The Country Doctor

one end of the horizon to the other, their arches touching the upper reaches of the sky. Often, they were present in half dozen numbers at the same time. To view such magic was like living inside a colossal kaleidoscope of color.

I disembarked from the plane and walked over to the two men who appeared to be waiting for someone. The administrator of the 35-bed Indian Health Service hospital and the attending Indian Health Service physician had volunteered to drive me to my quarters, ten miles away.

"We were expecting to see a very large man," Tom, the administrator, remarked after introductions had been made.

"Well, my name has nothing to do with my anatomy or my size," I replied. "People who see my name in print, HIPPS, sometimes imagine me as a man with two big hips that must belong to a very big body."

It was easy enough to become acquainted with the outpatient clinics and the emergency rooms of Indian reservations. Many of the problems were not unlike those I saw on a daily basis back home. There were broken bones, lacerations, respiratory infections, and skin rashes. In addition, there was diabetes, high blood pressure, heart and kidney failure--universal problems suffered the world over.

Alive and Well

"Wow!" I exclaimed as I examined the feet of my young 17-year-old patient. "How could this have happened?"

The bottom of each foot from heel to toe was one uninterrupted blister, filled to capacity, like a water balloon, with serous fluid. The lad's toes were indistinguishable from the rest of the foot, and his pain was intense.

"We just finished the five-mile foot race for this year's powwow," his companion explained. "Joey happened by just as it was about to begin. He had no shoes on, but he said he could run even faster in his bare feet."

I still cringe with sympathetic pain every time I remember that boy who won the race and the one-hundred-dollar prize. Those blistered feet were quite a price to pay for victory.

Now, there's a strikingly beautiful young woman, I said to myself as Laura walked into the clinic. She was one of three contestants I examined for their competition in the year's annual Miss Native American Beauty Pageant. She lit up, not only the building, but the entire reservation with her presence.

My physical examination found not the slightest of defects in the young lady. Hers was a smooth skin with a

The Country Doctor

bronze complexion of the most wonderful kind. Laura's smile, her poise, her carriage, her personality, every aspect of her body language, was totally charming. Everything about her exuded perfection. I knew beyond any doubt that I had just met the next Miss Native America, USA.

Summertime on Indian reservations meant wildfires in the prime forests west of the Rockies, and that meant fitness examinations for the healthy, strong, younger men who were eager to respond to the government's call for firefighters. I was quick to learn that they did not sign up for the thrill of fighting fires, but rather for the love of a well-paid job. After six weeks, they were pleased to return to their reservation homes as the village big spenders for as long as the money would last.

Like anywhere in the country, some Native Americans, especially adolescents and young adults, could be a reckless and scrappy bunch come the weekend. Saturday night in the Emergency Room was usually a challenge. Injuries and several other problems were often alcohol related.

I recall one very-intoxicated, young man who presented himself with genital complaints and the pain, burning, and discharge of a venereal disease. What mildly astonished me was that he could not remember where and when he had been exposed, whom his partner had been, and whether he'd actually engaged in sex. But his male anatomy knew for sure.

Now, this is the most colorful celebration I've ever witnessed, I thought as I viewed the passing parade of floats. Each one seemed to outdo the one that had preceded it. Proud-looking braves on horseback, with headdresses flowing to the ground, and costumes of the most brilliant style and color, were complemented by their magnificent stallions, similarly decorated with elegant harnesses.

It was the first week of my stay on the Blackfoot reservation in Browning, and the parade was heralding the country's annual powwow celebration. Authentic teepees decorated acres of land. Indians came from dozens of reservations across the country. It was a delight to experience the powwow, the highlight in the lives of those descended from our country's native ancestors.

The powwows did not resemble flea markets nor weekend carnivals by any means, nor were they week-long county fairs. They lasted for weeks, enabling everyone to enjoy the wide and exciting variety of entertainment. Dancers were elaborately costumed, and throughout the

The Country Doctor

affair, Native American chanters provided a continuous background music.

A mood of admiration and a deep sense of history permeated the place. Artists with paintbrushes, musicians with banjos, and craftspeople with bead work of the most delightful kind were there in great numbers. All in all, it was a spectacular experience for everyone, a bejeweled oasis in an otherwise nearly trackless desert.

I witnessed once again, and from very close up, the "Great American Disgrace" from many points of view. After country doctoring in a half dozen clinics and hospitals from the Dakotas to the Rocky Mountains, it became apparent to me that the Native Americans were one of the country's minority groups. This awareness increased as I became personally acquainted with their socioeconomic plight in the country's overall scheme of things.

I felt disappointed to see political corruption among their own leaders. Those remote reservations were not immune to the universal game of greed, money, and power. Self-serving leaders had learned to play the game well. They had the best of all role models back there in the white man's federal government, back there in a place named after the father of our country, Washington.

Alive and Well

I left each reservation remembering much about the people forgotten by the federal government and the nation. Promises made to the original owners of our country, the Native Americans, in the beginning and ever since, seem to have been the most forgotten.

Politicians can be like babies in diapers;
they need to be changed often and for the same reason.

Interlude 11

Acutupps

The success of acupuncture, long promoted as a means of treating a wide variety of human ills, has led to the acceptance of acupressure and acutouch. Both are descendants of the original acutreatment.

Acu-, meaning needle or sharp, has taken on the tenor of sudden, quick, or light, indicating that touch and pressure have become a part of the caregiver's healing hands.

Acupuncture penetrates the skin by means of a thin, sharp needle to a point where the tip brings about relief of pain and heals disease. It is a method that seems to work for a lot of people with whom success cannot be denied.

Less invasive is acupressure, a placing of the hands over a painful muscle and application of firm pressure without rubbing.

Acutouch, the gentle placing of fingertips on a throbbing headache or a painful joint, has worked for all of us more times than a few. Remember, it worked for us as infants and children when mother patted our aching hearts and kissed our boo-boos.

Chapter 12

Hills of Home

Nostalgia isn't what it used to be.

At the time, I felt deprived. After all, it was a Saturday afternoon, a picture-perfect October day, and two of my brothers and I were in a mountaintop cornfield. Three miles away, down there in the valley, sat my little hometown. The sounds of the high school marching band and cheers from the crowd at the weekly football game distracted my attention from the chore at hand.

We were sharecropping. For every three bushels of corn we shucked from the stalks, we earned one for ourselves. It was field corn, of course, and we used it for feeding our pigs, fattening them up for our winter's supply of ham, bacon, sausage, shoulder roasts, pork chops, and tenderloins. That thought, along with the threat of my father's hickory stick if we didn't cooperate, was the driving force for our work on the hill.

This is hill farming at its toughest, I thought, looking around at the nearby open meadows. There was no such thing as a flat field in the area, only rolling hills with slopes of varying grades. In order to plow, one had to

The Country Doctor

make semicircular arcs from one side to the other. The cows and horses grazing on the slopes seemed to tilt uphill in order to maintain their balance. Men and boys did the same.

I remember when I left the country to enter the Navy during World War II. I had been chided about my roots. My fellow sailors were quick to say, "We can tell you're from the mountains of Appalachia. You have one leg shorter than the other."

Later on, when we were aboard ship on the rolling main, I chided them back. After all, the hill country had equipped me with sea legs that enabled me to walk straight and upright in the roughest of weather.

It took a half hour each morning to climb to the hilltop from home. We had a front-row seat for the dawning of each new day. Beyond the open fields was a 360 degree vista view across hills and valleys as far away as some 40 miles. It was possible to see the ridge tops of seven surrounding counties from that special place.

In dawn's early light, fog fills the valleys between companion hills with a caring gentleness. A magical world emerges around my place on that very high summit. Where the tips of the summits pierce through the dense cloud cover, the scene resembles a vast ocean filled with a myriad of floating islands.

Alive and Well

As the sun appears above the distant horizon, there is a quiet kiss of affection as the mist touches the dancing waters in the streams meandering through the valleys below. The mystical ground clouds ascend ever so slowly, hugging the loins of the mountains with tender caresses. As they move upward, they embrace the trees and snuggle with bushes and grass and wildflowers. They blanket wildlife in maternal comfort. Just before they let go of their mother Earth, they break up into pale, white, muslin-thin wisps and patches that cling to and flutter around the hills like angel fairies sipping nectar from the tree tops.

It is a perpetual blessing, both in the light of day and in the darkness of night, when my view, unencumbered by the sights and sounds of humankind, is filled with only this earth and sky. A cloudless night is as clean and pure there as anywhere in the universe. A hilltop night-watcher can see forever into the past, right up to the present, and on into infinity through the windows of star-bright skylights.

When mountain country seasons slowly and surely change from autumn into winter, the land disappears under a thick blanket of snow and the hilltop becomes a winter wonderland. Long, smooth slopes, many with their foot a full mile from the crown, are the perfect place for

The Country Doctor

tobogganing. The drop is close to a thousand feet, and that means speed!

During my childhood days, my skis were handmade at home with a single, one-inch strap that held my foot to the board. Balancing poles were unheard of. The trail was a shush-boom, straight down the slope. I did my best not to lose a single ski on a slope such as that. It would be a long walk down and back to retrieve it.

The only shortcoming of that wonderful place was the absence of a tow rope or a ski lift that would have transported us from the bottom to the top. A one-mile walk in deep snow was one great fitness event.

Our homemade "go-devil" gave us the greatest thrill. It was an equally great challenge to ride. A four-foot barrel stave was used to make the ski. A sixteen-inch-high, four-inch-wide log, placed two-thirds of the way toward the back, was topped with a wooden seat four inches wide and twelve inches long to complete the rig. The trick was to maintain balance, aim our rig straight down the hill, roll back and forth a few times, and go like the devil. Of course, the steeper the slope, the better. It made for a quick start. The faster it went, the easier it was to stay upright.

Alive and Well

As I grow older and "wiser," I occasionally reflect on how tough life must have been back then, in the depressed years of the 1920's and 1930's. I realize, too, that childhood, for anyone is always a challenge. At the same time, it can be interesting, exciting, and happy. Even some sixty years later, I can say that I would not have traded mine for any other. To be a child is to be totally absorbed in every moment, and that means fulfillment all the way along, whether or not the family be affluent.

Childhood, for me, was indeed a miracle of survival. In a family of nine children, there were only two broken bones over the fourteen years we lived together under the same roof. There were no major illnesses, nor were there any operations. No wonder I have nothing but enthusiasm and optimism for life and living.

My only remembered illness as an older child was probably a summer virus. My recollections of the several days I was ill and confined to bed are of the great, mouth-watering chicken soup and special treats brought to my bedside by the folks who lived next door. Neighbors were like that then, much to my mother's appreciation and my own pleasure. It was almost enough to make me want to remain in bed a little longer than necessary.

The usual childhood diseases plagued our large family, especially since the children were aged eighteen to

The Country Doctor

twenty months apart. We went through a cycle every two years with regular measles, German measles, mumps, chickenpox, and scarlet fever. That was the norm in those days before preventive vaccines were available.

For the duration of the diseases, a 12" x 16" quarantine sign would be posted by the front door of our home, warning all of us to stay inside and everyone else to stay outside.

Considering the incubation period of each of those maladies, that sign was put to frequent use. One of us would no sooner get over the quarantine period of two weeks and be ready to return to school, when the next youngest would fall ill. It was the rule that as long as one of us was sick, no one in the family was permitted to leave. Thus, we were kept homebound for several months every other year.

My older brother really enjoyed those school-free, family epidemics. He could hardly wait for the next one to come along!

You know you're getting old when you've lost the child inside yourself.

Interlude 12

A Final Fix

Bleeding from the nose is usually caused by irritated mucous membranes on the septum separating the two nasal passageways. Such irritations are caused by cold weather dryness, virus and sinus infections, scratches, and bumps, all of which can rupture the small capillaries. Bleeding, for the most part, is slight and sporadic.

Prompt stoppage happens with firm pressure on the bleeding side by pressing the nostril against the septum. Hold the nostril for a half minute or so, then repeat as long as necessary. A few minutes is usually all it takes. If the bleeding does not stop promptly, cold compresses over the nose and face can help.

Don't depend on ice cubes on the back of your neck to stop the bleeding. Your nose is just too far away from your neck. On the other hand, it's a good way to make a numbskull of yourself.

Chapter 13

Miracle Child

A child in the home fills all the corners.

Polly was just two years old when I first met her. For me, it was love at first sight. The instant I saw her pretty face, I knew she was something special. The twinkle in her eyes and her sweet smile were captivating. At her very young age, she glowed with a personality that instantly caught my breath short. It was more than just her looks. It was a poise that struck a confidence to her bearing. She sat at the end of the examining table with no trace of fear, brimming with self-esteem.

Polly's mother, a single parent receiving welfare, first brought her to the office because of a fever and a sore throat. Over the years, I was to see Polly every few months for minor things. Occasionally, we would meet on the sidewalks or at the grocery store. She never failed to greet me with that perpetual smile, her confident poise, and a wave of her arm. No matter the circumstance, Polly was never without her charm.

In my mind, I saw her as a precious wonder. And yet, that miracle child lived with her mother at the poverty level. She had no siblings, she had no father. Polly had

Alive and Well

been deprived of many of the material things other children take for granted. In those many ways, she could have been looked upon as a social misfit. Nothing in her biological or social background seemed conducive to a desirable atmosphere in which she could prosper physically, psychologically, and spiritually. And yet, Polly did. Indeed, she did.

It was my day of the week for rounds at Memorial Hospital, twenty-five miles from my office. When I stepped into the elevator and pressed the button for floor number five, I came face to face with a year and a half old child, unquestionably a boy, snuggled against his mother's chest.

We looked at each other, and his face lit up with a smile as broad as his little cheeks allowed. His eyes sparkled brightly. I kept looking away, then back again, and each time the smile flashed on as though from the snap of a light switch.

Several peek-a-boos later, I left the elevator with a great big smile of my own. His was still there, too quickly disappearing behind the elevator door.

Heidi enriched my professional, as well as my personal, life each time she visited the office. To see her name on the schedule was to know it would be a bright and beautiful day. When blonde-haired and blue-eyed, three year old Heidi entered the front door, her special

The Country Doctor

glow filled the entire office. It lasted long after she was gone.

In addition to her personality, she had an enchantingly-intelligent manner of speech. She would recite nursery rhymes and sing fairy tales like a professional, little genius. It had to have been a very special gift, just as Heidi was.

As with special people the world over who master foreign languages with ease or possess the gifts of superior intellect, mathematical genius, or photographic memory, those children--my patients and my eternal friends--have a large dose of celestial ingredients in their genetic makeup.

One of the many nice things about being human is to know fellow beings who possess the soul of a saint, the voice of a nightingale, the wisdom of a sage, and most precious, the confidence and esteem of special children.

Could it be that the unlimited dimensions of outer space are, in effect, one vast reservoir of ingredients for molding human lives--body, mind, and soul? Those ingredients are there by the grace of God for individuals as they go and come, die and are reborn again. They are available for new life and are brought together with the crossing of male and female vectors at the instant of conception. In this way, they are providing each of us with our unique individuality regardless of to whom we

Alive and Well

are born, in what part of the world we live, or the social circumstances of time and place.

Babies and little children are natural experts in speaking the universal language of body posture, facial expression, and sound. They kick with delight and scream in pain. They speak loudly and plainly with a smile and a laugh and a twinkle in the eye. There is no doubt of their message. Adults use body language, too, though with increasing inhibition as they grow away from the spontaneity of childhood.

And yet, people the world around, no matter their race or color or creed, their country or politics or religion, possess mutual understanding and acceptance in the language of music and dance, a wave of the hand, an embrace, and a smile.

I remember Polly's personality, Heidi's charm, the smile of the elevator child, and the universal language with which we spoke.

What does a bee sound like when it's flying backward? Zzub zzub zzub.

Interlude 13

A Blessed Trinity

A professional athlete may be physically perfect. A college professor may be mentally complete. A hermit may be out of this world.

Most of us are a mixture of physical, mental, and spiritual parts. Optimum life is best achieved with a reasonably equal amount of all three.

And, it is humanly possible to be in meaningful balance between all three no matter who we are, where we are, and what we do in this world.

Chapter 14

Harmon's Little Acre

Gentle sympathy needs no words to be felt.

Harmon's place was less than half an acre. It was a one hundred by two hundred foot plot of ground near the dike of the town's small lake. It was situated in the flood plain of spring's winter runoff and summer's thunderstorms. No one else would live in the dilapidated, old frame house except my patient. He had no choice. It was the only place in town he could afford. Its surroundings were a stir fry of overgrown weedy grass and decrepit old trees.

Harmon, with his grizzled prematurely aged appearance, seemed the appropriate resident for the shabby little house with matching landscape. Undernourished to skin and bone and with a slow and painful walk caused by two artificial knees that hadn't taken well, he was living his last few months of life slowly succumbing to cancer of the lung.

His pride and joy was a yard overcrowded with broken-down tools and several pieces of lawn equipment which, like Harmon, had lost their power and mobility. He took great pleasure in tinkering with them anyway. I always listened intently as he told me what was wrong with one after another and what he figured was necessary to put them back into operation. It was a ritual at every visit, and I became well acquainted with each machine during the first summer I made my house calls to Harmon's little acre.

On the other side of the dike was lovely Mirror Lake, created thirty years earlier at the confluence of two pristine mountain streams and sired by the United States Army Corps of Engineers. It was built to serve as a flood control dam for downstate Pennsylvania. At the same time, it became the crowned jewel for Susquehoning, an otherwise simple Allegheny Mountain town which nestled in seemingly endless mountains that pleasure the senses for all seasons. Ridges are tall and steep with these valleys sensuous and deep. They embrace the body and soul of visitors and travelers as well as permanent residents.

"This is a very beautiful scene," I remarked as Barbie and I strolled along the lake's shore one dark and starlit night.

"That it is. It's cozy and quiet and definitely romantic," she replied, wrapping her arm in mine.

"Well, I can't help but agree with all those nice adjectives," I whispered in her ear.

Bright lemon-colored wild iris glowed along the banks, the night sky twinkled in agreement, and we lingered long.

Such walks unwound us from our unusually busy schedules and brought us back to the sweet reality of daily life and living. We appreciated the changing scene as wildflowers, from the woodland violets of spring to the asters of autumn, graced the pages of our days. Around the lake on warm, sunny afternoons, butterflies were like mobile flower gardens. Birdlife became rainbow confetti in the early mornings. Together, we were a special duet, loving each other inside a beautiful symphony.

It seemed incongruous that these two scenes, the lovely lake and Harmon's tumbled down shack, were within a hundred feet of each other. By fortune or design, the dike obscured one from the other for the casual observer and the passerby. One could not see both at the same time without standing on top of the dike.

Of course, the lake and those who viewed it didn't care for Harmon's plight any more than he did for the lake. It made no difference to the city dwellers sixty-five miles south, where the crystal-clear Hickory Creek headwaters flowed into Central Pennsylvania's scenic

The Country Doctor

Susquehanna River. Nor did it concern the people who cast their lines into the deep pools of one of the country's best trout streams.

One day, Emma, Harmon's wife, had stopped by my office and asked that I go to the house to see him.

"He's getting weaker steady along," she had explained. "Can hardly walk or even stand. He's dizzy all the time. Seems like he's slowly dying."

The following day as I climbed the steps to his porch, I was startled by a loud snore. It was a hot and humid summer day. I had not expected Harmon to be there among the clutter that crowded the porch leaving only a narrow walk space between the steps and the front door. The entire porch was littered with a hodgepodge of broken-down furniture and appliances. My patient blended into the scene as a natural part of it all. The sight had the feel and the smell of a fly-infested day.

Harmon was sprawled back to a nearly horizontal level on what was left of a lazy man's chair. His grey, bearded head faced the ceiling. His feet rested on a foot stool, and the rest of his body hung suspended in between. I looked closely for a moment to see if he was still alive. After that last snore, followed by a deep gulp of air and some convulsive twitching of his body, I was not sure. The flutter of a few whiskers of his mustache gave him away as a small jet of air escaped from his mouth.

It was fascinating to watch passing flies stop to hover over Harmon's face. They were alternately breathed into his wide-open mouth, then out again. A hapless one disappeared down his throat never to return. I knew he had swallowed it by his short, quick gulp and a smacking of his lips. The others could not quite make it in against the force of his expired air.

When Harmon felt my presence on the porch, he slowly raised his lids just enough to peek at me with sleep-glazed eyes. Eventually, he recognized me and weakly raised a limp hand in greeting.

Inside the large, one-room, living quarters, there was minimal evidence that three other beings were living there. Emma's decrepit brother, Tim, and her mentally-impaired daughter, Florence, were staring blankly at a mid-afternoon soap opera on television. Emma was at the table having a cheese and cracker snack. She barely acknowledged my presence. I wondered if she remembered her visit to my office just the day before.

"This is midsummer's day dream time," I thought, as visions of Erskine Caldwell's *God's Little Acre* drifted through the eye of my mind.

I often wondered about the stench of some of those back-country places where people live their lives of quiet

The Country Doctor

desperation. I could never quite identify the exact ingredients of that unique odor. Stale and unhygienic, I finally decided it must be the result of a peculiar mixture of unbathed bodies, unlaundered clothes, and a mysterious variety of other things.

Over the weeks that followed, Harmon became bedridden, weak and wasted by his deadly disease. Emma called me one last time, begging me to visit him and give him a shot to relieve his pain. There was an unspoken plea in her voice that it be a strong enough dose from which he would not awaken.

Wracked with unrelenting pain, he was, indeed, the epitome of impending death. Sadly, I remembered Harmon's tales of his earlier years. He had been an accomplished musician in the heyday of his life. Over the years, although he had not played with great orchestras, he had made a living as a versatile multiple instrument player with a number of small bands.

As I stood at his bedside for what I thought would be the last time, I did not expect to cure Harmon of his disease. His plight caused me to reflect once again on a favorite thought for the caregiver of one's fellow human: I am here to cure when possible, relieve when I can't cure, and comfort always.

An average dose of Demerol® would have been a heavy dose for Harmon's weak and wasted body. Yet, his pain was severe. Common sense and compassion measured out the proper dose, which the patient took without a whimper in what was left of his buttock's muscle.

The next morning, Emma called to tell me that Harmon had settled down and slept peacefully after my visit. Sometime during the night, he had passed away. He had played his last tune.

I sensed the unspoken gratitude in her voice that I had granted her wish, that I had given him a lethal dose. I decided it was all right for her to think it, knowing that I had not. I felt, along with her, content to have relieved his suffering.

Time doesn't go--it stays. It's we who go.

Interlude 14

Memory

Complaints of poor memory have been so common in my forty years of medical practice, I have trouble remembering how many times a day I hear them.

Occasionally, loss of memory is an important symptom, indicative of serious physical or mental illness and requiring study and treatment.

The majority of time, forgetfulness, or the inability to remember something or somebody, is due to fatigue, distraction, pain, headache, or one of many transient and treatable conditions.

If this complaint is a common one for you, consult with your professional caregiver. If it's decided that you have no serious problem, relax, and keep in mind: The next time you have trouble remembering, it's nothing serious. Just forget it.

Chapter 15

Sweet and Low

Sugar and spice is not always nice.

Jerry was a hard-working, hill farmer and, like most, he was no dummy. As I listened to his story, he made the diagnosis an easy one for me.

"I can tell you it really bothers the devil out of me, Doc!" he said. "These sudden spells of weakness and dizziness, this queasiness in my stomach, it's enough to knock me off my feet. I just can't keep up with the farm work.

"Here I am, 6 feet 2 inches tall, 220 pounds, and as strong as an ox. Usually, I can work from dawn to dark," he went on, "non-stop except for meals. Most of the time, I can carry an ox on my shoulders while I work like a bull to care for the cows. And, there are a hundred other things to keep up with since Harley had his stroke. I'm doing the job of two, and it's getting worse. The symptoms are coming more often and lasting longer."

"Jerry," I said, "you've got hypoglycemia. That's all. Nothing serious, just something that can bother you if the symptoms get bad enough."

The Country Doctor

"Well, you can tell me it's nothing serious," he replied, "and I believe you."

"And I believe you," I responded. "I know that when the sugar gets low enough, it can lay the strongest of us low."

"Tell me more about it so I can understand what's going on. I want to know what I can do."

"It's like this, Jerry. We all have a certain level of sugar in our blood. It's what gives us the energy to live and work with every day, beyond just sitting around, sleeping, and doing little else. Sugar must be maintained at a certain level in the blood-- not too high or we develop diabetes, not too low or we have hypoglycemia. The level depends on the food we eat which turns into sugar after we digest it into our systems. The insulin our bodies produce helps to metabolize that sugar into energy.

"If we don't have enough insulin in our system, then diabetes develops. It can be treated by controlling the intake of carbohydrate foods and by supplementing insulin, either by injection or with insulin substitute pills.

"When the sugar gets too low, it's important to control stress as much as possible and to avoid sugar-rich foods. Stick to a protein-rich diet and eat smaller portions of food more often. It helps to eat food at regular meal times, then have a snack at mid-morning, mid-afternoon, and bedtime. This doesn't mean you need to eat more each day, just that you should spread it out over the day. Hypoglycemia spells usually occur about two to three hours after eating."

"Yeah, Doc. That's right!"

"That's because when you eat, a portion of the food becomes sugar in the blood. In turn, the pancreas secretes additional insulin to burn up the sugar and cause your sugar level to drop. That's when the symptoms hit. And, that's why you need to curb sugar-type foods in your diet and why you should not go too long without eating."

"Okay," said Jerry, "I think I understand that well enough. Now tell me what I can do about it."

"I pretty much have, Jerry. Watch the carbohydrates in your diet, and take your food six times a day instead of three. More than likely, you will lose those extra thirty or forty pounds over the next six months, and you'll feel all-around better for it."

"Is this thing for real, Doc? This hypoglycemia?" Jerry asked.

"I do know some people, some of them doctors, who don't subscribe to the idea. They just don't give it the credibility it deserves, and they pass it off as an imaginary thing. It's much easier for them to ignore it and write it off as a psychological something they claim exists only in your head.

The Country Doctor

"Now that you and I have discussed this, I will prove it by running a glucose tolerance test on you. Then, you and I, together, can decide what to do about it. You know how you've been feeling and whether this applies to you. I know I'm satisfied with my history and examination of you.

"You don't have some dreaded disease and you're not losing your mind. It can be fixed. You're going to feel normal again and stay that way as long as you follow my cost-free prescription of watching your food intake."

Jerry chuckled. I knew he was smart enough to do the right thing for himself, and he did. Over the following months, he gradually improved. He lost his excessive weight and stabilized at his normal 180 pounds. Occasionally, he visited the office for an update and some counseling about his diet and lifestyle.

One day he revisited the office in a state of urgency. His symptoms had suddenly worsened. Their frequency, severity, and duration had become intensive. He was near panic, so we talked about his situation in greater depth.

"What is it, Jerry?" I asked. "What's bugging you besides work and diet?"

"All is not well back on the farm," he replied wearily. "Since Harley had his stroke, I've had to do more and more of the chores. And, I'm worried that I'll have no part in the inheritance of the farm. It's my wife's family's farm, you know. And you also know that small farmers have little or no health or disability insurance. Our incomes are just too limited to make any provisions for retirement. Here I am, forty years old, working my fool head off just to get by from one day to the next."

More than Jerry knew, I understood his dilemma. His concerns were legitimate. There was certainly more to cope with than his workload and his diet. His spirit was being consumed by the unfairness and the uncertainty he felt about his situation.

It was easy for me to identify with Jerry and his constant struggle to survive. He is the last of a fast-fading breed of small-family farmers struggling with a multitude of overwhelming odds. He's not unlike the family doctor. I wonder how much longer it will be possible for me to practice out of my small office with only a few pieces of equipment and a blend of endurance, compassion, and good low-tech medicine. It is fast becoming a romantic vision of a golden age. Is the faded black bag doomed to extinction like old-time movies and so many other things that enrich our lives?

Doc: How are you doing today, Jim?
Jim: Oh, about 50-40.

Interlude 15

How Low Is Hypo?

Much of the time the doctor and patient are dealing with hyper things: hypertension, hyperthyroidism, hyperactivity, hyperacidity. The world in which we live is a high-pressure, excessive activity place. There is too much of so many things.

We have become so familiar with hyper things, it can be easy to overlook the hypo things. These low-down conditions often are just the opposite of their hyper counterparts. Low blood pressure, for example, is common but not as dramatic or life-threatening as high blood pressure. Nevertheless, hypo conditions are significant to the patient who suffers from them.

Hypo means low. The more common hypo conditions are low blood pressure, low thyroid metabolism, low blood sugar, and low blood count.

The bottom-line symptoms of hypo conditions are the same: loss of energy or pep, lack of endurance, drowsiness, light-headedness, listlessness, and lack of interest in life and living. Mental alertness and clear thinking also decline, and physical activity lessens.

Alive and Well

If you experience one or more of these symptoms, it may take some help from your doctor to put the finger on which condition is affecting you. This can usually be accomplished by a visit to the office, a basic physical examination, and occasionally, some blood testing.

Remember, also, a few simple and fundamental facts. Mental attitude can put you down physically as well as mentally. Lack of physical exercise gets to you because of that fundamental principle for all living things: Move it or you'll lose it!

In order to avoid the rustiness of arthritic joints, human beings are meant to move, and the body is meant to be used. All parts of us--the skin, heart, lungs, joints, nerves, brain, and intestines are self-lubricating, but only when used and moved.

Chapter 16

Jack Spratt and Millie

*If you can't laugh at yourself,
you're in serious trouble.*

Millie and Roy Johnson had welcomed me into their home once a month for several years, but as things turned out on that particular April morning, I wasn't sure how welcomed I would be. My arrival was a bit out of the ordinary.

The southern slopes along the road leading to their old, white, frame farmhouse were filled with a sweet awareness of life. The leftovers from last year were few and far between. Dark-brown seed pods of cat-o'-nine tails had changed color to a fluffy light tan. They resembled large, wooly caterpillars about to shed their insulated underwear that would become a part of the new year's bird nests. The rains of the prior few days were nourishing an explosion of wildflowers. Streams were washing away the litter of winter's waste and flushing the hills and valleys into another Allegheny springtime.

Alive and Well

As I stopped at the end of the bridge leading across the stream to their farmhouse, I slid out of my Chunker to listen to a red-winged blackbird vent his early spring call. Something moved in the pool beneath the bridge, and I went below to have a look. I spotted a half dozen native brook trout. Fascinated, I watched them drifting back and forth with the current. They were speckled with red and brown. The scene brought back to mind many a camping and fishing trip when, fresh from the stream, the catch was pan fried in butter until golden brown and, in no time, melting in my mouth, bones and all.

I leaned over further, trying to take a closer look when . . . SPLASH! . . . swoosh! . . . Suddenly the trout I had been watching from the rocky ledge were swimming around my head. We were all gasping and bubbling at each other as fins and arms and legs moved back and forth in a kind of erratic ballet.

Now, mountain stream water is always cold, even in the middle of summer. In April, it is downright numbing!

Drenched and purple to my chattering teeth, I sloshed across the floor of the Johnson porch grumbling about losing my footing.

The Country Doctor

"I heard you coming," Millie said, "but I didn't know what you were." Her eyes grew wide and round and her chuckle let me know she would be talking about the incident for years.

"You're all wet! Where have you been?"

"Out cavorting with some of our native trout," I answered. "May I stand over your register?"

She hustled me inside, ignoring the puddles I was leaving behind.

In the center of the living room was a large metal grate about four feet square. A delicious draft of warm air rose through it from the wood furnace located directly below. The warmth felt wonderful, though I was a little disconcerted at the ominous sight of the red, glowing furnace head just beneath my feet.

I was standing there, deeply content, musing over the day's happenings when Roy came in from the barn. The old man stopped motionless in his tracks while he watched the water from my trousers drip through the grate under my shoes as clouds of vapor enveloped me.

"Now Doc, I've got these extra clothes of Roy's," Millie chattered as she re-entered the room. "You just change into them till ya get back home. You can use the bathroom, right here."

Alive and Well

Eighty-year-old Millie had an indomitable spirit, a lively sense of humor, and some cherished idiosyncrasies that kept her on top in the face of many a physical adversity. In fact, she was a big package of multiple diseases--high blood pressure, diabetes, heart disease, and arthritis. She was tall and heavy, a Mrs. Jack Sprat, with pretty snow-white hair. Her black-rimmed glasses tipped the end of her nose just as they had before she became a retired school teacher. Her kitchen counter was always a treasure island of home-baked cookies, cakes, and sweet breads. Her baking was seasoned with a generous dose of Yankee philosophy, "Eat it up, wear it out, use it up, or do without."

She specialized in the "eat it up" part, which guaranteed her a problem with overweight. The sweets and excess weight were the worst possible medicine for her diabetes, but for Millie, not eating heartily was something akin to not going to church.

Dressing quickly, I came out to be greeted by Roy's belly laugh at my Charlie Chaplin look. His six-foot-four-inch frame pants were cuffed up a good twelve inches on my legs. His forty-two-inch belt around my thirty-inch waist gave me little sense of security.

The Country Doctor

I was reminded once again why house calls were my favorite way of practicing medicine. They got me away from the confines of an office. I relished seeing my patients in their own surroundings and loved the lightheartedness of our combined company. They got me out into the countryside for close-up glimpses of the natural world I love so well (including close encounters in a cold mountain stream).

Millie's toenails needed trimming that day, something I did for her about once a month. She could no longer reach her feet and toes. Yet, she knew how important foot care was, for diabetics are at risk of poor circulation in the legs and feet and infections from minor scratches and bruises. Millie had learned the lesson well from her own mother, also a diabetic, whose leg had been amputated many years earlier for just that reason.

As Millie wiggled and squirmed across the bed for her nail trimming, she reminded me, "I have a lot of pain and a lot of body to pain." I didn't dispute that as my one-hundred-forty-pound body confronted her own two hundred thirty-five.

Roy, eighty-two years old, was himself an amputee. A Jack Sprat at six feet four inches and one hundred seventy pounds, he had lost his leg some fifteen years earlier. An auto accident had crushed it so badly that it had to be amputated at mid-thigh.

I became well acquainted with Roy's leftover limb over the years. Although he no longer had a leg, he occasionally experienced phantom pain which, for him, was a burning sensation in the foot that was no longer there. It was caused by irritation, pressure, and scar tissue on the sciatic nerve at the end of the amputated limb.

A strand of nerve tissue resembling a cable that normally goes down the leg from the back to the foot was the culprit. It still had a memory trace in Roy's brain of where it used to be, and it would send pain signals back to his head from time to time. An occasional injection of novocaine and cortisone gave him relief for several months.

Each time I trimmed the nails of Roy's right foot, I remarked about how fast they grew. He reminded me it was because all of his body's toenail energy went into one foot. Roy's toenail story was a treat every time he told it as I listened and chuckled at the picture that formed in my mind.

For the past fifteen years of his working life, he had tended to the residents of a nursing home. Once each

The Country Doctor

month, after a bath that softened their nails, the residents would stretch out on their beds for a toenail marathon. Roy and his co-worker would set to work and trim all 2,100 nails, on 210 sets of toes, on 105 pairs of feet. Afterwards, they swept up the trimmings and scattered them as compost on the nursing home's vegetable garden.

Both Millie and Roy were specialists in old-time story telling. Over the years, those two seasoned characters filled many of our hours together with one story after another.

My visits always ended with the three of us sitting around the counter in the middle of their spacious country kitchen. Tea and coffee topped off a generous snack.

"Care for cream?" Millie asked as she passed me a can of evaporated milk.

My eyes fell on the three big letters on the label. I had not seen nor touched a can of PET milk for a lot of years. I remembered my mother's kitchen, holiday cookies on the table, and PET milk in the cupboard.

The three of us sat together for a spell on that April morning, like old neighbors do. We traded a few more stories between Millie's and Roy's periodic gentle

Alive and Well

skirmishes over whose turn it was to wash the dishes or do the laundry.

If I could be a mouse in one of the many corners of that old house, I would be witness to a lot of serious, but loving, contests that poked at each other's foibles as they vied to see who was the sicker of the two.

I went on my way after a while with a throat full of heart-felt gratitude that those dear people would welcome me into their private lives. I admired their art of embracing their own misfortunes and showing how well love and humor can transcend pain.

"By the way," said Roy as he let me out onto the porch, "next time try using a pole to catch those fish. You won't get so wet that way."

*Two trout are dining in a restaurant
when one of them starts waving
his empty glass in the air.
The waiter turns to the busboy and says,
"I think there's a fish out of water at table three."*

Interlude 16

Target Organs

A target organ is that part of the body that is affected by injury, disease, or stress. It can also be a part that is the end-point of a test or treatment, as in chemotherapy for cancer.

You know you have a target organ when stress of any kind affects a part of your body often or in the same way; i.e:

- When you get a cold, it usually settles in your middle ear, sinuses, throat, bronchial tubes, or lungs.
- When you are allergic to pollens or dusts and the like, it affects your eyes, sinuses, nose, or bronchial tubes. In one case, it is called hay fever and in the other, it is asthma.
- You are sensitive to a particular kind of food and your skin reacts with eczema or hives. Your stomach may also be the target as a gastritis, and the lower bowel as a colitis.

Alive and Well

- You do strenuous physical work as a part of your job and your lower back is weak and painful much of the time.
- You get excited or upset or you do something physically strenuous and you get chest pain.
- You are under pressure or mental stress and you get a tension headache or a migraine-type headache.
- You are not careful with your diet or you overindulge in smoking, alcohol, or highly seasoned food, and you get heartburn or recurrent ulcers.

It is helpful for you to know your target organs, to realize what agitates them. When you do, you can learn to prevent flare-ups. You may, also, know when to see the doctor so that the two of you can decide what you need and when you need it.

For example, you may know from your past experience that what may seem like a mild, virus, head cold for the first two or three days always settles in your sinuses or lungs and that you end up needing antibiotics.

When familiar with your history, the doctor can better understand your diagnosis. Your treatment will be quicker, better, and less expensive when you both know what's going on.

Chapter 17

In To Africa

To perceive something is one thing; to experience it is quite another.

Through a doorless opening on one side of the room to an exit on the other, a steady stream of natives made their way across the dirt floor, stopping for a few minutes while I looked at each one long enough to try to decide what was wrong and what to do.

In that flood plain of the Upper Nile River, in the South Sudan of Central Africa, I was armed only with my stethoscope, otoscope, and bandage scissors. The small, thatch-roofed hut was devoid of windows, light, and water; and I felt more than a little ill-equipped to handle the line of nearly three hundred sick and injured people. I would need a large dose of country doctor sense to see me through the next few months.

It was a silent parade of shadowy, slouching figures of all sexes and ages moving slowly along in zombie-like fashion. They were thin, weak, skin and bone, obviously undernourished, and sick with a wide variety of tropical diseases. Everyone in that hot and humid bush country existed at the tattered edge of life, ravaged by at least two or three major conditions within one body all at the same time. It ran the gamut from leprosy, tuberculosis, typhus and dengue fever, malaria, small pox, and tropical ulcers to a multitude of skin infections and parasitic diseases of every imaginable kind.

It hadn't taken me long to see where all those maladies came from. Waste disposal was on the ground, right when the urge struck to move bowel and bladder. Both animals and humans shared that unsanitary means of elimination.

Waste from domestic animals was collected in piles of various sizes here and there and anywhere. The dried cakes were used for cooking fires in the grass and mud huts. They were, also, used by the children who picked up the material, be it wet or dry, with their bare hands, and threw it in snowball fashion at each other. Their aim was for a direct hit to the head, an accomplishment achieved with great glee.

Everyone lived with a multitude of infectious parasites, viruses, and bacteria in, on, and around them as a constant part of everyday life. Those organisms were present in the mud and food, on the clothes and skin, everywhere.

When I had spent time in the laboratory of a hospital in Ethiopia the year before, every patient admitted had

The Country Doctor

their stool checked for parasites, just as back in the States we routinely check for anemia. Everybody had not only one, but two or three different kinds of infectious parasites as a routine finding. I was amazed that any of those tragic people could survive at all.

In Sudanese bush country, there was no such thing as a well-baby or a whole-health clinic. The sole "clinic," in which I was to practice, served some ten thousand natives from small villages which were scattered over many square miles in Upper Nile River country. That's all the medicine there was.

I had expected more in the line of equipment and supplies, not realizing my destination was a bush country clinic. Its remote location dismayed me, being dozens of miles and many hours away from the nearest hospital and accessible only by river boat. How I wished for my black bag and all the wonderful things it contained.

I thought of the differences and the similarities between that day's roster of patients compared to a day in my office back in Pennsylvania. In some ways it was the same. Many people suffered simultaneously with multiple diseases such as high blood pressure, diabetes, arthritis, and heart disease. Those patients, too, were miracles of survival. The difference in Africa, although the conditions were no less multiple, was that they were more acute and less forgiving to life. Those suffering souls did not last long. The death rate at birth was fifty percent, children of all ages died of infectious diseases at a frightening rate, and the adults did well to live beyond the age of forty.

More than a few times I reflected on my medical school days when the textbooks identified their conditions as "exotic," meaning that they existed only in the tropical areas of the world. Later, I realized that some of the diseases were not so "exotic" after all. There were reports of scattered cases of leprosy in the southern part of the United States as well.

In more recent times when AIDS became the latest scourge to humankind, my African experience of the 1970's did not seem so remote after all. The occurrence of multiple infectious diseases, death at an early age, and living death while life lingers leads me to believe that AIDS did, indeed, originate in that part of the world. I don't believe it began as a sexually transmitted, drug related, or homosexual thing, but rather as a development of a badly weakened immune capacity in people ravaged and weakened by overwhelming odds. I suspect I was in the delivery room of the world where AIDS was born.

The Country Doctor

As a throng of ailing people crowded about me each day, I was comforted with the knowledge that I had left the United States with a complete battery of preventive vaccines for myself. Influenza, yellow fever, typhoid and paratyphoid fever, diphtheria, cholera, tuberculosis, and plague injections bombarded my body the weeks prior to my departure for that medical missionary adventure.

I would have taken others, but there were no others available. Added to all the immunizations was a whopping-big dose of gamma globulin to protect me from infectious hepatitis. (The development of the hepatitis vaccine was not yet in the picture.) My personal first aid kit was well supplied with chloroquine to ward off the threat of malaria. I felt fortified, much more so than thirty years before when, during World War II, as a bell-bottomed sailor, I had sailed away to the islands of the South Pacific.

A little boy, eighteen months old, was clinging to his young mother's flank. His face was swollen in front of and below his ear. Feverish, fussy, crying, and eating poorly, he obviously had a severe case of mumps. According to a microscopic examination of his stool specimen, his diarrhea came from, not one, but three different kinds of intestinal parasites.

Alive and Well

His mother, equally sick, had a large lump in her neck that had burst open from the pressure of an internal abscess. The lump's ulcerated surface was oozing a bloody pus that slowly dripped down her neck onto her shoulder. I had not seen a case of active tuberculosis of the lungs since my medical school days and had never seen tuberculosis of the lymph glands. Thirty years ago, that infectious scourge was rapidly losing its death grip on hundreds of thousands of people around the world, but not there.

The little boy had at least one good thing going for him. Clad only in a loose-fitting blouse that covered his little body to the waist, his bare bottom was clean, healthy, and free from any sign of diaper rash.

My mind occasionally drifted back to the months prior to my trip when I had gotten medicine samples from every drug company I knew. Aspirin, Tylenol®, antibiotics, skin creams and ointments, decongestants, antihistamines, sulfa drugs, and pain relievers were collected by the thousands.

For easy transport, my church group's Sunday school kids had helped to condense them from a great number of small packets to large plastic containers. The collection had weighed in at two hundred pounds and, along with one suitcase of personal items, was my

The Country Doctor

constant companion as I left New York City for Paris, Rome, Cairo, and finally Khartoum, the capital city of North Sudan.

The last leg of my journey had been by a twin-engine cargo plane. The seats had wooden benches lining both sides of the fuselage. Everyone's baggage had been tied down in one great pile in the middle. I literally perched myself on the top of the boxes of medication for the entire journey to prevent them from being lost to the black market, never to reach the desperately- needy natives of the bush country.

From the airport in Upper Nile Providence, my baggage and I then completed the trip in an outboard motorboat. I traveled about forty miles up the White Nile to the Sobat River tributary and then penetrated further into the lush, tropical bush to my final destination. It was there at the Doleib Hill mission that I was to spend my time attending the sick and injured.

Missionary Ken Alexander, his wife, and their three children were struggling to reintroduce Christianity to the natives of that part of the African continent. It was the Presbyterian Church's first attempt to evangelize the people since the country had gained its independence

Alive and Well

from Great Britain in 1957. Wednesday and Sunday church and school meetings were held. Also, their mission conducted a training course for local natives who wished to become Christian pastors to their own people.

Prior to its independence, the region had been partially Christianized by Ken's father. Following independence, the Arabic North and the multiple native tribes of the South launched themselves into a bitter civil war.

The conflict lasted for seventeen years during which time all of the schools and churches of the South were destroyed by pillage and fire. In turn, the natives lost their Christianity.

And, who is to say those peaceful, nature-loving people were not just as spiritually well off on their own.

Twelve-year-old Chad looked like a little old man; his face was drawn and hollow-eyed. Emaciated by hookworm disease of the spleen, his abdomen was swelled as though pregnant with child. He simply looked at me. Neither he nor any one of the others made any demands. They had no requests, just a quiet pleading in their eyes. The silent cry of a badly undernourished body said it all. I knew that when I returned to that place the following year, Chad would not be there to see me.

The Country Doctor

After two weeks in the missionary school compound, the day came for a pilgrimage up the Sobat River to the next village, forty miles south of Doleib Hill. Ken Alexander made occasional visits to the other villages in the region in his attempt to extend his Christian outreach just a little bit farther.

Upon arriving at each location, it was interesting to see that I received a more enthusiastic welcome than Ken himself. The natives were so anxious and so needy for medical help, that they came to me first.

Two weeks earlier, when my plane descended into Khartoum, I had my first view of the Nile River. The Blue Nile, after thundering out of the Ethiopian escarpment from the east, joins the muddy, meandering White Nile that flows out of the South Sudan and Central Africa. From their confluence, the Nile then flows through Egypt to empty itself into the Mediterranean Sea at Cairo.

The farther south one travels on the White Nile to the Sobat tributary and into the heart of Central Africa, the more serene and more beautiful the land becomes. Although I arrived in the rainy season, most of the time the sky was clear and filled with billowing white clouds that accentuated the striking azure backdrop. Lush foliage bordered the river's edge and appeared to extend unendingly over the flat land of the Sud, even farther than

Alive and Well

the eye can see. It was a first-prize, picture-postcard scene. If I ignored the one-hundred-degree heat, the ninety-five-percent humidity, and the hoards of pesky disease bearing insects, the beautiful view was, indeed, a serene and pristine experience.

Bird life was abundant and amazing. As our outboard motorboat struggled slowly but surely over the sluggishly flowing surface of the plant-choked water, we seemed lost in an unending sea of tall, thick tropical grass. Periodically, from over the billowing waves of grass, a large, dense flock of birds appeared like a thick cloud momentarily shadowing out the sun.

Thousands of small-sized warblers moved in a single mass with great, undulating speed, disappearing as quickly as they had came. Very tall, slender, long-legged cranes stood along the riverbanks looking like stalks of reeds. Slowly, and with seemingly great effort, they rose into the air as our boat traveled by, just barely getting off the ground by the time we passed. Pelicans, despite the awkward and burdensome appearance of their large, boat-like bills, soared onto and off the river's surface as gracefully as high-tech, mechanical aircraft.

The surface of the Nile and its tributaries abound with lush, light greenish hyacinths that float in clumps of varying sizes. A lovely pale-blue flower blossoms out of each clump, mirroring the beauty of the sky above. The plant grows profusely, living only from the water and its nutrients, reaching a proportion of several yards in width. It is not unusual for those floating islands to grow so thick, so tightly together, that it becomes extremely difficult to navigate even a small rowboat at bends and narrow sections of the river.

There is always the danger of becoming lost in that floral forest of the flat, slowly moving river with no detectable current. It took experienced natives to make it through. Watching them navigate, I imagined that each one accomplished this amazing feat with a built-in compass at the end of the nose.

Floating islands, as the natives call them, were compressed in great numbers into large, round, tight, raft-like boats that served for human and freight travel. As I enjoyed the exquisite loveliness of each individual plant, I marveled that something so delicate could serve such a purpose.

A twenty-five-year-old native man, mentally and physically normal in all respects except for the hallmarks of his infirmity, came up to me after we entered the village. The cartilage of his nose had been destroyed, giving it a typical, camelback saddle shape. The skin of his face, arms, and legs were marked with the lumpiness of various sized and shaped leper nodules at the tiny nerve endings. His fingers and toes had parts missing--varying from tips on some, ends on others, and for others, the entire part.

Of the many tropical diseases I had ever heard and read about, probably the most mysterious was leprosy, that strange and dreaded disease so vividly recollected from the lessons of my childhood Sunday school days. Supposedly confined to the tropical and subtropical regions of the world, its victims were ostracized from society and confined to leper colonies to prevent the spread of the disease. That isolation practice reminded me of how, in the first half of the twentieth century, United States tuberculosis patients were similarly banished to a sanatorium.

It is not the lepers' germ, *mycobacterium*, that produces the dramatic destruction of fingers and toes and their spontaneous amputation. Rather, leprosy damages the nerves, resulting in numbness and absence of pain. Burns, bruises, cuts, and abrasions, readily healed by uninfected individuals, become repeatedly infected. Gradually the nails, bones, ligaments, tendons, and muscles are destroyed and drop off as the process goes on and on.

I learned that leprosy is not as contagious as tuberculosis. Yes, it can be spread to others by intimate personal contact, but it is manageable by medication and medical attention. Supervision is necessary to ensure that treatment continues long enough to bring about remission and prevention of infection. The victims, therefore, can live in society just as those who have cancer or a host of other disease conditions.

As we traveled back to Doleib Hill that day, I reflected again on the question of just how effective efforts really are at Christianizing the native peoples of Africa, Asia, America, and elsewhere. It seemed to me that it would be necessary to improve the quality of life in the third-world countries with the development of better transportation, communication, sanitation, food, water, and health--at least to the same degree as religion.

Within two weeks of my arrival, I had used up the 200 pounds of medicine I had brought along with me from the States. I wondered what I was to do during my remaining time there. The most I could do for some was to listen and look for a few minutes and wish for a whole lot more.

My mind frequently burned with the question: Was life so cheap back in the jungle that all too quickly it was written away and that small efforts such as mine amounted to little or nothing?

As I left to attempt my re-entry into life back home, I decided it was not. The lines of little funeral processions that appeared frequently and briefly as a gently moving part of the African landscape convinced me that even in that primitive bush country, life and death somehow had significance.

Laughter is like a smile; it has no foreign accent.

Interlude 17

Potpourri

Potpourri is pronounced, "po-poo-ree." It means a collection of things, usually herbs, flowers, or berries in small containers which are placed in a room for fragrance.

Chicken broth is said to combat sore throats and colds. Actually, any hot soup will do. It is the hot fluid that nourishes you, increases the flow of mucus over the membranes, and makes it more difficult for viruses to cling to healthy cells. Campbell's and chickens really have nothing to do with it.

Regardless of your age, baby oil is one of the best lotions for dry skin. It's great for body massage as well.

Chapter 18

Jenny's Zoo

*Cheerful people resist disease better than the glum ones;
it's the surly bird that catches the germ.*

By the calendar, spring had arrived exactly two weeks earlier, but it was not until the very day I headed for Jenny's place that the weather caught up with time. I could see, hear, smell, and taste it as I journeyed those eight country miles that would bring me close to the headwaters of Hickory Creek. In one brief moment, all my senses experienced the change from the tail end of winter to the front end of spring.

The morning fog was beginning to slowly leave the valley on that cool and pleasant day. Only when the sun appears over the ridge top is the fog willing to creep up the loins of mountain slopes. It takes until mid-morning before the last traces reluctantly let go to become the cloud cover of afternoon.

A mourning dove, perched on the naked limb of a nearby maple, yearned with a plaintive coo for his mate. Tending to her freshly laid eggs, she was hidden in a white pine tree just a short distance away.

The Country Doctor

Doves are birds of love who mate for life and are seldom seen without each other. Unlike most other birds that sing their song of courtship until eggs are laid and hatched, the male dove woos his mate all summer long. Inspired by each coo of that fellow in the sweet maple tree, it was easy for me to feel a deep love for all things, especially for my own special sweetheart.

Jenny's yard was a dull grassy green at that time of year. I knew that in a few weeks, I would receive my annual gift of dandelion greens. I was looking forward to that. Her yard grew a heavy crop of the golden-yellow flowers that were accentuated by rosettes of tender, succulent blades of top-rate salad makings. With anticipation, I would wait for my first grocery bag full two visits from this one.

As I turned into the driveway, I was confronted with the stark reality of the reception committee. Each time I visit, a canine chorus begins the instant I start up the drive, increases in volume when I cross over the yard, and intensifies to the limit as I knock on the door. I feel as if I've arrived at a vet's office or the zoo.

When I knock on the door, six dogs leap up to the window, all at one time. It's always a relief that the door is closed as twenty-four paws pound against the door and six sets of jaws take turns at the window.

Alive and Well

After what seems like several minutes of wild commotion, Jenny commands the dogs to be quiet, to "go and lay down." As the canine chorus diminishes to an occassional yip, I hear her voice calling, "It's okay, Doc. You can come in now!"

My black bag always precedes me into the house. Its size is a comforting shield between me and all those vicious sets of teeth.

Gradually, the noise stops and the dogs find one place or another to settle down. From time to time, there is a sniff at my pant leg and black bag. Even after numerous visits, I continue to find it amazing that two people, six dogs, three cats, two uncaged parakeets, and one gerbil have enough living space in a small, four-room cottage.

The three cats assume strategic locations around the room. The Siamese usually sits on her haunches, about two feet from the ceiling, atop a six-foot chest of drawers. She appears to be there as the uncontested monarch of the menagerie.

The calico continually roams about the room. Her head moves from side to side in a mild state of restless agitation as if she is searching for the appropriate place to settle in, unsure that there is one.

The black cat's head is seen at the lower corner of a doorway. It is the most noticeable due to a pair of yellow

The Country Doctor

eyes that stare at me without blinking. Occasionally, he will show his sharp white teeth in a manner that could be interpreted as either a crooked half-smile or a cross-toothed snarl. I am careful to keep my black bag between that cat and me.

The dogs are more difficult for me to recognize as distinct personalities. Their greeting at the door and their constant scampering, slinking, sniffing, and scratching after I once get inside unnerves me. I gave up trying to call them by name after the first few visits. Besides, they are not the patients I've come to see.

As always, I found 29 year old Marsha seated in her wheelchair. She is unable to talk because of advanced cerebral palsy, but she speaks loudly and clearly with her cheerful face and a very big smile. The palsied exaggerations of her head and upper trunk movements have taken on a joyful expression and her friendly greeting matches an indomitable spirit within. Although she has no control of her voluntary muscle movements, she is in complete command of her thoughts and feelings.

In fact, it is Marsha who remembers to tell me of any new complaint she and her mother have had since my last visit. She is also quick to remind Jenny about the prescription refills they need.

Alive and Well

Communication between those two has been fascinating to watch. Marsha space writes to her mother with slow, awkward movements of her arms, spelling out words in the air for her to read. It is equally interesting to watch Jenny read the words backwards as they are spelled out until a complete sentence comes together as a meaningful idea. It's like watching a silent moving picture in reverse and slow motion.

While the diaphragm of my stethoscope rests on Marsha's chest, I playfully place my hat on her head. She chortles and laughs as I remark, "You're so much better looking in my hats than I."

The left upper chest is the best place to check her pulse, for it is clearer there than in the wrist or the neck. It is, also, the place to listen to each of the four valves of the heart when checking for particular malfunctions due to such conditions as congenital heart disease, rheumatic fever, mitral valve prolapse, or degenerative and arteriosclerotic conditions.

With the earpieces of my stethoscope adjusted to fit snug in my ear canals, I can minimize outside noise interference.

I've been grateful that when I first learned to use my stethoscope, I did so to the background medley of jackhammers, saws, and hammers while the University of Pennsylvania's School of Medicine underwent construction

The Country Doctor

of bigger and better facilities for patient care and teaching. At the time, I doubted that it would be possible to learn to ignore all kinds of background noise, including the cry of a baby and the scream of a child. It was a matter of learning to focus on that which was important for a doctor to hear. Since then, I have been a better listener in all kinds of ways.

When I use a stethoscope today, even though forty years have elapsed, it is seldom that I don't recollect second-year medical school days in the class of physical diagnosis. It was my first time away from the textbook, the classroom, and endless lectures by one professor after another. It was my opportunity to hear and see for myself what I had previously only read about.

Physical diagnosis comes after a history of the patient's complaints. The first and most important part of dealing with health and disease is to talk with and listen to the patient. Then comes the physical examination, the looking, seeing, and listening with the aid of a stethoscope, blood pressure cuff, and thermometer. The laying on of hands follows. Then, blood tests and x-rays and more elaborate high-tech tests, such as CAT scans and MRIs of the modern medical scene. Short of a ruptured appendix, gallstones, tumors, and the like,

Alive and Well

surgery was, and still is, only an occasional remedy when all else fails.

I am more convinced today than ever that a proper history of the patient's complaint and the physical examination can take care of ninety percent of all health problems. And yet, tests and special studies routinely done, whether they are needed or not, can amount to about ninety percent of the cost of medical care!

In the meantime, I was attempting to ignore the sniff of a wet nose at the stethoscope diaphragm on Marsha's chest. The dog on her lap seemed as curious about the diaphragm as I was about the sound of the valves between the upper and lower chambers on the left side of her heart. I heard the usual murmur of a mitral valve prolapse, a condition in which the valve is extra loose and doesn't stay closed as it should with each beat of the heart. As the heart goes through its regular pumping cycle, there is a to and fro leakage of blood. When severe, the problem can weaken the heart over a period of time and lead to congestive failure.

During each of my visits, Jenny insists on knowing not only her daughter's blood pressure, but also, her own. She had been trained at one time to be a nurse's helper in blood pressure screening programs. She was proud of that connection and kept in touch by way of remembering

The Country Doctor

the limits of a normal reading. The symbols of her nostalgic experience are kept in her dresser drawer--a cuff that no longer works and a stethoscope that is no longer used.

A blood pressure of more than 150/90 was always a concern to Jenny, so it was not uncommon for me to fudge the reading down a few points when it read 152 or 155. White-coat, high blood pressure is very common. Many people's pressure will be elevated just because it is being taken. Such people, who really have a normal pressure, will suffer the effects of too low a pressure if treated with medication. In order to be accurate, it is important to take readings two or more times in both arms in an unhurried manner.

I once again assured her, "Jenny, your pressure is quite all right. You don't need to take medicine for it. It will only make you feel bad. Do the basics and the simple things first. Keep your weight down. Be careful of too much salt in your diet. You've got to get some exercise, too, you know. We've talked about that more than once. Do the best you can to keep mentally and physically relaxed. When you're able to do that, like a good percentage of people, medicines just won't be necessary."

As I hugged them goodbye, Jenny suddenly exclaimed, "Oh, just a minute, Doc! Don't go yet. I want to show you the latest addition to the family!"

Alive and Well

She rushed into the next room, and I expected her to bring out a picture of a new great-grandchild. Instead, she returned holding a very young kitten in her hand. It was one from a litter of five born of her very old cat, Granny. Jenny was concerned for the mother and hoped that would be her last litter.

"She had a hard time delivering the kittens, Doc. Had to take her to the vet. Just couldn't do it on her own."

I scratched my head in wonder about another addition to an already crowded household and said, "Well, there's nothing cuter than a newborn kitten, unless it's a puppy."

Every dog has its day--but the nights belong to the cats.

Interlude 18

Vitamins or Not

Medical fads, like all kinds of fads in today's world, come and go. It is unfortunate that some happen in the first place, and a celebration when some go as fast as they came. A perpetual one that seems to be infernally eternal is the use of vitamins and minerals.

It has been a popular one during my entire 40 years of practice and fluctuates from A to Z. No sooner do amino acids make the news and profit for its promoters, than zinc pushes it out of the spotlight. Vitamins B, C, D, and E come and go along with beta carotene, antioxidants, and melatonin.

It is a simple truth that vitamins and minerals are not routinely necessary for the average healthy person. Another truth is that most of us get all we need if we eat a commonsense, regular diet. The less we take in that's not natural, the better.

The supplemental vitamin and mineral industry is a multimillion dollar a year business in the United States alone. Where are the most benefits seen? In the body, in the bathroom plumbing, or in the bank accounts of those who make, distribute, and sell the products?

Despite the changing attitude of health professionals that sees health supplements necessary because of the effects of pollution, soil depletion, food additives and preservatives, and stresses of all kinds, keep in mind many foods from the marketplace are already variously supplemented.

Aim first for a commonsense, well-balanced diet. Maintain a normal weight and stay fit by a moderate amount of exercise. If you are fit, nature will help you to help yourself and you won't need all that superfluous artificiality.

Chapter 19

Hill Farming

Gill tells me he knows when it's going to rain by his knees--if they have water on them, it's raining.

"Do you like red potatoes?" Gill asked, as we chatted back and forth during his regular office visit for arthritis in his knees.

"Do I? Well, you know that's like asking kids if they like ice cream or cotton candy," I replied. "When it comes to spuds, you bet I do!"

"I have a hundred-pound bag in my trunk you can have. It's left over from last season, and I'm getting ready to plant the new crop."

Gill had an unusual way of talking, quick and curt with frequent humpfs and grunts scattered throughout his speech. The clarity of his pronunciation sometimes got lost in the undulating staccato of his sentences. He underlined a word now and then with a forward nod of his head to make a point. I figured that came from a lifetime of talking to his work horses, long before the appearance of tractors on the all-American family farm.

Alive and Well

"Ya know, Doc, you've been treating my knees for two years now. We both know it's the degeneration kind of arthritis. The x-rays proved that. My elastic cushions are wearing thin," Gill tumbled on. "I can feel the end of my bones grinding against each other, and that's pain! You've helped me some with your commonsense advice and medicine. I don't feel as bad as before, but that's not as good as I want to be.

"I want to keep workin' my potato farm, ya know. I've been doing it all my life. It's been my livelihood and my family's daily bread for forty years. I don't want to give up yet."

"I know how you feel, Gill," I said with sincere compassion. "I wish I could do more."

"I just don't feel good enough to do what I want to keep doing," he continued.

Gill's farm is a 1,000-acre, mountain-country Shangri-la. It sits on Blueberry Ridge, which is divided into two major drainage systems that flow separately into the Susquehanna River sixty miles south of the farm.

As I drove my Chunker off the top of the ridge toward the bottom, Gill's farm appeared almost unexpectedly to my right. Tree-covered hills and many

The Country Doctor

sections of open field stretched out in all directions. They were not the flat fields of the usual potato farm, however. The various sections tilted in a multitude of degrees and directions, conforming to the lay of the land.

It is, indeed, a special mountain country place. I can readily get in touch with Gill's love for that land. Most of the trees had been removed from the slopes of the higher ridges years ago. Green fields and pastures patterned the land like a crazy patchwork quilt. The whole scene seemed to be nestled in the half-opened palm of Mother Nature's well-worn hand.

It is understandable that Gill's knees gradually gave way to the stress of tilling that ground for his beloved red potatoes. He had spent many a year high-stepping in and out of countless miles of furrows behind a two-horse plow, long before the tractor added a new kind of horse power to small family farms.

Coronary bypass surgery had slowed Gill down for a few weeks two years ago, but his knee problem was persistent. The pain was constant, and he was not about to have an artificial joint operation.

In spite of the mountain's uneven and irregular terrain, the biggest and most popular of Laurel County's farm crop is potatoes. Their high quality found them regularly boiled, baked, mashed, fried, marketed, and consumed all over the country. There was no question that Gill's red ones were the cream of the crop, and when it comes to spuds, to not like them would be like disowning Idaho and Ireland.

"You know, Gill, you're seventy years old now, and you've been working these slopes for a long time. How much longer do you want to keep it up?" I asked.

"Well, I've been gradually cutting back on my acreage these past five years," he admitted. "I'm planting only six acres this year, and that's down from sixty in my prime."

"It's too bad none of the boys are interested enough to keep the farm going," I reflected, "but that's a common story these days, isn't it? Many of the single-family farms scattered far and wide around here and throughout rural Pennsylvania are long gone. Some have simply been abandoned and allowed to grow back into woodlands."

"And there's no changing that!" Gill exclaimed. "I've tried to get the boys to stay, but we all knew it was a lost cause a long time ago.

"Anyway, I want to tell you how my knees have been doing for the past month. About a month ago, one of my flatlander friends from downstate was at my place for deer hunting. I was telling him about my arthritis. He came close up to me and, with a hushed voice to my ear, said, 'Let me tell you about a cure for it,' He kept looking around furtively as if no one else should be privileged to hear his secret.

"Then he told me, 'I just heard this from my eighty-two-year-old grandmother. It completely cured the arthritis that she suffered with for forty years.'"

"All right, Gill," I said kindly, curious to learn about one more of Granny's home remedies. "Tell me what it is. You know I'm always willing to learn about Mother Nature and her cures."

"Well, it's Certo®," he grunted.

"You mean the thing that's used to make jellies and jams!?"

"Yes," he rambled. "Ya put one tablespoon in a glass of grapefruit juice and take it once a day. I've been using it for a month now and my knees are a good fifty percent better. It's better than any medicine you gave me."

"You sound convinced, Gill. I can't disagree with that kind of success."

It is not possible to live and practice medicine in rural America without hearing about such home cures.

Alive and Well

Doctors are a prime target for these secrets. It's as though people like to let us know there's something and somebody else out there other than ourselves that can cure people's ills.

I've wished more than once I could get the attention of some of my patient's as effectively as the curbstone experts do. It seems that such "experts" get better compliance with their customers than I do with my patients!

> *"It's your gallbladder, Joe,*
> *but if you want a second opinion,*
> *it's your kidneys."*

Interlude 19

Fatigue

Fatigue, along with headache, insomnia, and pain is one of a handful of the most common complaints that plagues humankind. It can mean anything from tiredness to lack of pep, listlessness, weakness, or lack of endurance. Both doctor and patient may find it tricky to put the finger on one cause out of dozens of possibilities, but the first step is to decide if your fatigue is natural or unnatural.

Natural fatigue can be due to loss of sleep, overwork, lack of physical and mental exercise, overweight, excessive smoking, alcohol, drugs, or television. Usually easy to diagnose, it is often more difficult to treat since it is lifestyle determined and requires individual responsibility to overcome it.

Unnatural fatigue may be caused by physical or psychological disease. Physical causes can range from acute illness to cancer. Psychological causes can range from boredom to mental illness.

When you can't sort out the problem by yourself, your doctor should be able to help by examination and testing after a half hour or so of asking and listening. If your doctor won't or can't give you that kind of time, find one that will.

Chapter 20

Snow Birds

A closed heart gathers no love.

"You are the director of this race for the United States Snow Shoe Association," Connie declared in no uncertain terms.

"What!?" I exclaimed. "Do you know what you just said? Why, there's no more than a handful of people around here who have ever been on a pair of snowshoes. Most people have never even seen a pair except in pictures! How will I get enough participants to pull it off?"

"Well, you said you were interested in the sport," Connie responded curtly, "and you know Greenville better than I do. You are a full-fledged member of the U.S.S.S.A.(United States Snow Shoe Association), and you are the Pennsylvania representative."

"Hmm, now what?" I muttered into my chin. "How am I going to do this? What am I to do?"

That question was frequently on my mind over the next few days. It was the middle of November, and the race was scheduled for the first week in February.

The Country Doctor

A new patient entered my examining room the next day, and before she left, she entered the snowshoe race as well as my life. Over the next few months, that office visit became more and more memorable and the snowshoe race became increasingly more possible and more important.

That was Barbara's first visit. She was a total stranger to me as we went through her medical and family history and examination for her complaints. Her work experience piqued my interest as did everything else about her. My ears perked up like a rabbit on the run when she told me about working with the State Parks and Forest Service for a number of years.

"Barbara," I asked. "you don't by any chance know how to snowshoe, do you?" I knew I had more than a hint of excitement in my voice.

"Why sure," she remarked with a confidence that took me more than a little by surprise. Her pretty blue eyes sparkled as she spoke about her work on snowshoes with the annual elk herd survey in north-central Pennsylvania. She told me of her trail work and the pleasures she enjoyed from our beautiful mountains in the snow. "Why do you ask?"

By that time it was difficult for me to keep from shouting for joy and dancing a jig. It was even more difficult to keep from hugging her and kissing her on the cheek. Of course, that was not the expected or the accepted thing to do in the doctor's examining room, especially with a new and unknown female patient.

"Barbara, would you be interested in helping out with a snowshoe race this winter?" I could hardly contain my growing enthusiasm.

"What do you want me to do?" she offered, in that same matter-of-fact manner of which I was to become increasingly appreciative and fond.

This is just too good to be true, I kept thinking to myself. "Can this be so?" I asked. "Are you sure you're not the good snow fairy and I'm just dreaming? When the door closes after you leave, will you disappear into thin air? Are you sure?"

Lifting her big blue eyes in smiling assurance, she inquired, "When do we get started? I'm ready to know more about it."

My composure quickly returned and my breathing came back to normal. "Right away. There's a lot to do over the next two months. We need to raise money and promote the race. We must quickly stir up some interest, and we absolutely must have some participants. Some snow would help, too!"

The ensuing two months saw a flurry of activity, not the least of which was a hope for snow flurries in time for

The Country Doctor

the race. Saturday and Sunday afternoons became snowshoe school days. Local businesses and organizations responded with contributions for the purchase of snowshoes for all interested novices. Snowshoe awareness in the immediate and surrounding area added another dozen participants, along with experience.

Snowshoeing, of course, is not a new means of human ambulation. It's been around since humankind has walked upright in those parts of the world where snow falls and accumulates a few inches or more. The shoes themselves have changed quite a bit, however. A great variety of sizes, shapes, and materials have been developed to accommodate the renewed interest of a large number of people.

The essential requirement of a snowshoe is that it be wide enough and long enough and have a narrow frame. Within the frame is a network of webbing that sufficiently distributes the walker's weight and prevents the person from sinking more than a few inches into the snow. So that the shoe will not catch in the snow, a turned-up tip is part of the design.

Walking is unexpectedly easy and quick to learn. The basic rule is to lift the forward-stepping foot high enough and far enough over the stationary shoe to avoid

Alive and Well

stepping on it. It is not necessary to waddle-step. A normal gait, just slightly longer than the usual walk step, is all it takes. The many other minor tricks come from a little practice.

The race was an official U.S.S.S.A. race, and the rules were specific. In those early years of organized snowshoe racing in the United States, races were conducted in the snowshoe states throughout the northern, western, northeastern, midwestern, and northwestern regions. The winners of those races competed for national championships where they could qualify for what would eventually be International Olympic competition.

Our small, but official, race in this part of Northcentral Pennsylvania, seemed a big order and a long way from delivery. Early on, there were no more than a half dozen pairs of snowshoes in the county, with the same number of experienced individuals.

Not to be discouraged, we scurried right down to the day of the race. The official track was properly laid out, the snow was packed, and the raceway and finish line were flagged with official starters and timers. Three heats for each of the three events--the 100-meter dash, the 400-meter dash, and the mile-long distance run--were carried out in official fashion. A grand total of thirty racers arrived to participate. There were children and adults, novices and veterans, all ready and eager to run what had seemed an impossible dream eight short weeks earlier.

Not surprisingly, Barbara went from teaching novices about the wearing and caring of snowshoes to becoming a star participant on the day of the race. After two falls during the dash events, she quickly recovered to win the one-mile, long-distance run. With her combined time in all events, she finished as the number one snowshoe race woman. At the same time, her performance and her charm melted the hearts of the spectators and other participants, including myself.

There is no doubt that one must see a snowshoe race to appreciate the fun and the spectacle of this unusual and challenging sport. Snowshoe walking is one thing, easily accomplished with the aid of ski poles for balance and push. Running is another matter. One needs strength, endurance, and high-step prowess. Like a miniature cyclone, waves of snow fly off to the sides and in the wake of each runner.

To witness a fall is to see a flurry of arms, legs, snowshoes, poles, and snow. To be the victim is a very personal experience.

I predicted back then that when snowshoe racing became an event at the International Olympics, it would quickly become a well-watched favorite. And so it happened, much to the delight of the spectators and to

Alive and Well

our own amazement. From a small beginning, bred and born in little events like ours, international snowshoe racing was on its way.

As soon as our north-central Pennsylvania race was over, plans for the next year began to smolder in the minds of the organizers.

The following year was even better. There were more participants and more spectators. A new brand of triathalon was added to the events. The official race was climaxed by a one- mile snowshoe race, immediately followed by a three-mile, cross-country ski trek, and then a six-mile foot race. And that was ten miles of a special kind of endurance.

Exercise is good for the heart--especially when it's hugging and kissing.

Interlude 20

Morpourri

After forty years of practice, it has been a learning experience to realize that about ninety percent of people with a new, physical complaint try some form of self-treatment and get better because of it, or in spite of it. The remaining ten percent visit a health-care provider.

Cold compresses are good for treating any kind of itching skin rash. It's an old favorite--safe, effective, inexpensive, and free of side effects.

Sour cream is a simple and effective remedy for sunburn. It's easy to obtain and simple to use. After applying, leave it on the skin for one to two hours, then rinse off in the shower with tepid water. Repeat every few hours as long as necessary.

Chapter 21

Tincture of Time

Disease is biological; illness is behavioral.

"What's up, Harley?" I asked. "I haven't seen you since one of your horses squeezed you between its hind quarter and the side of a stall three years ago and fractured three of your ribs."

"I am in *s-e-v-e-r-e* pain," he replied.

For him to say that, I knew he was in trouble. He showed it, too. Harley was never much of a complainer. It took something very physical to get to him. He was saying a lot with his body language. His arms were dangling loosely in front of him and his face was contorted in agony. To see him was to feel the intensity of his pain. I noticed, too, that he was trying not to move his head or take a deep breath for fear of aggravating his torment.

Sometimes it's a trick and a challenge to evaluate a patient's pain. It begins with a series of questions to myself. Is pain present at all or is the problem an ache or a discomfort? Is it mild or severe? Does the individual's reaction or lack of reaction to pain tell me whether or not it's serious?

To make sense of it includes assessing the victim's personality. If I know the patient, the task is an easy matter. If I don't, I rely on my experiential intuition. Whiners and groaners are one type, stoics and tough-guys another.

Harley was obviously feeling intense pain. Words weren't needed to confirm that. He was not a huge man, but he was heavily muscled and very strong. At five feet ten inches and two hundred pounds, I faced him at five feet four and one hundred thirty pounds. Normally he could have picked me up by the nape of my neck with the tips of his index finger and thumb and set me on a shelf as far up as he could reach.

"What happened to you, Harley?" I asked. "Where is your pain?"

"I was on the job two weeks ago," he said. "I was picking up a tractor-trailer truck wheel to put on the balancing machine. I twisted to the left to get it in place and felt a sudden stabbing pain in my back. I didn't come in sooner. Just couldn't believe it would amount to much."

"Show me exactly where it is."

Alive and Well

He followed my fingers to a spot in the middle of his upper back just to the right of the spine. I placed my index finger on the ligament between the knobs of two vertebrae halfway down from his neck and pressed firmly.

He was quick to react with a loud yell and a quick withdrawal. The menacing look on his face caused me to reflect on how easy it would have been for him to set me up on that shelf.

"Aha!" I cried out. "This is an easy one! You tore the ligament between these two vertebrae. It's like turning your ankle hard, or your knee. If it's not torn too badly, it should heal all right over the next few weeks."

"Few weeks!" Harley shouted. "But I want to go back to work tomorrow. You've got to do something right now."

"Oh, I can do something," I remarked. "It's already taken you two weeks to get yourself into the office. That means some scarring is going on where the ligament was torn. I'll give you an injection of prednisone to stimulate healing, and I'll expect to see you back here in ten days."

"It's a little better," Harley related at his next visit. "About fifty percent. But I know I can't handle those 150-pound wheels. At times, the pain hits me quick, even when I'm just driving in my car. Are you sure you know what's going on? Why am I not getting better faster?"

The Country Doctor

"There's been more tear of the ligament than I judged," I replied. "It's not able to heal as quickly as we would both like. It's going to take longer than I thought."

"Well, how much longer?" he growled. "I wanted to get back to work three weeks ago. Can you do something to speed it up? What else can be done?"

"I'll give you something to relax your muscles and something for pain relief. The medication will help you sleep better and move enough to help recondition your muscles. Keep yourself up and moving. Exercise your back at the neck and waist. Stretch your upper back muscles by moving your arms and shoulders as far as they'll go in all directions. Do that at least four times a day."

Ten days later, Harley was no better and his patience had worsened as well.

"You've got to do something about this!" he demanded. "Are you sure of what's wrong?"

"I'm as sure as reasonably possible," I answered. "It still looks like a tear with scar tissue getting in the way, and it's going to take time."

"Well, I don't want to take time. I want to go back to work!"

Alive and Well

I realized I had lost his confidence. His impatience and his inability to work were too great for my reassurance to overcome. He needed a second opinion.

"I'll refer you to an orthopedic specialist. I'll make a call as soon as I can and get back to you tomorrow to let you know the doctor's name and the time of your appointment. I'll get you in as soon as possible."

Harley got no further with the bone and joint specialist who offered nothing more for diagnosis and treatment than I had. Over the next four months, he was seen by a neurologist and a neurosurgeon. He tallied up some thirty trips for physical therapy and another forty for chiropractic treatments.

The final step in such a case is to refer the patient to an independent medical examiner. This was done, and he recommended additional studies, including an MRI of the neck and spine, a CT scan and bone scan of the spine, and conduction studies of the nerves. It also involved another five thousand dollars worth of expenses, all of which resulted in negative studies. There were no ruptured discs, no pinched nerves, nor was there any bone disease. A last desperate visit for physical therapy mechanical evaluation of his spine confirmed the absence of all such possibilities.

The Country Doctor

"Now, are you ready to accept what I told you in the very beginning?" I asked. "It's been fifteen thousand dollars worth of doctor and test bills and eleven months of no work. You had a torn ligament.

"So, let's get on with getting you back to work at something you can do even though you still have pain. A torn ligament is something you can live and work with just as well as tens of thousands of other injured working people out there do.

"There is something you can do without undue suffering. You don't have to be a one-hundred-percent, all-American, tough guy who can lift up the back end of a tractor trailer with one hand and change a flat tire with the other."

Harley left my office for the last time just as he had entered eleven months before, arms dangling from stooped shoulders, head down, chin on his chest. It was no longer just physical pain. It was also the pain of a wounded self-image unable to handle the fact that his perfect, physical body had done him in.

Pain is inevitable; suffering is optional.

Interlude 21

Depression

Depression is another of the many emotional conditions that affect humans in their efforts to live in today's world. It is second only to anxiety and is said to affect some thirty million Americans at any given moment.

Feeling down or blue from time to time is a part of everyday living. If it passes quickly, it does not require treatment. Like anxiety, it needs medical attention only when it seriously interferes with normal work, sleep, meals, relationships, and the like.

Reactive depression results from an especially stressful event in your life such as the loss of a loved one, divorce, job termination, or prolonged illness. It is felt as grief because of loss, and sadness because of lack, of something important for good mental and physical health.

Certain diseases and medications can be the cause of depression.

Bipolar depression is the pendulous alternation of anxiety and depression.

Serious depression can be suspect in unexplained physical ailments such as indigestion, headache, fatigue, or nervousness. Other indications may be present in the

The Country Doctor

form of daytime drowsiness, nighttime insomnia, crying spells, impaired concentration or memory, feelings of guilt or emptiness or worthlessness, loss of appetite, excessive eating, agitation, listlessness, loss of energy and endurance, and recurrent thoughts of death and suicide.

It sometimes takes medical help to put the finger on the presence of significant depression and to determine its type and its best treatment.

If you feel you need help, don't hold back. You have a lot of company.

Chapter 22

Down on the Farm

A recently-discovered cure for idleness is called work.

    The all-American family farm definitely isn't what it used to be, I thought, as I drove my Chunker across the rolling hills of north-central Pennsylvania's Endless Mountains.

    Some of the farms have been bought up by downstate "flatlanders" as retreats to the wild woods. Many have been conglomerated into large, business-type farms. Others have simply been abandoned. Hay stacks have given way to bales or rolls encased in plastic wraps. Many of the old, wooden barns have fallen to rubble on the ground or have been torn down and replaced with long, low, metal buildings.

    What a loss, I mused.

    I remember the days of my youth and the summers spent on Grandfather's farm. There, and on neighboring family farms closer home, the ol' wooden barn was the focal point of fun and games. Stuffed to the roof with

The Country Doctor

loose hay, the mow was a magical playground. But, only for boys. It wasn't that we didn't like girls. It was just that parents, especially fathers, couldn't see their young daughters cavorting in the haystacks with playful young boys. I've since decided their concerns may have stemmed from flash-backs of their own haystack days.

And, play we did. There was hide-and-seek, through tunnels in the hay, from one part of the barn to the other and from top to bottom. Swinging from the mow was the ultimate thrill.

After freshly cut and dried hay came in from the fields in wagons filled to overflowing, it was lifted up to the roof on a large hook that looked like a giant, three-pronged, ice pick. One-inch rope on a king-sized wooden pulley carried the hay up and into the mows until the entire barn was filled to the rafters. After that, we could use the rope as a great way to swing from one side, across a wide-open space fifteen feet above the floor, to the other side some fifty feet away.

By the time I reached ten years of age, I had become a first-class, bare-handed cow milker. I could fill a milk pail in record time. Music was composed and played as milk squirted out of the cow's nipple onto the inside of the metal pail. That rhythm, along with knocking flies off the edge of the stalls with a sudden stream of white lightning, changed a chore into a circus event.

And, there was no greater excitement for a young boy than riding a plow-pulling farm horse, bareback in the good ol' summertime. Sixty years later I remember it well.

"But how can I get on?" I had asked, when my grandfather gave me permission. As a spry and short five-foot-two-inch, one hundred and twenty pounder, he was not much for lifting me five feet up to the horse's back.

"Well, I'll tell you how to go at it," he said. The perpetual twinkle in his eyes and the smile on his impish face was half hidden behind a handlebar mustache that extended out to each ear. How well I made use of those handles when I rode his shoulders as a toddler. They kept me from falling off as we frolicked around the house.

"See that half door over there? It opens up to the bottom level where the horse stalls are. It's where we throw forkfuls of hay to the livestock below. One of the horses is under the opening right now. You can slip right down onto his back for a ride."

As I let go of my hold on the edge of the floor, I found myself on the back of a raging bull instead of the expected

The Country Doctor

gentle plow horse! In no time at all, we raced out of the barn straight into the pasture at breakneck speed. In even less time, the bull suddenly stopped and I flew through the air with the greatest of dis-ease. I landed on the ground, scurrying for dear life to get over the fence and away from that snorting, red-faced, hot-tempered, long-horned beast that was hell-bent for my buttocks!

I think back to my first summer on the farm. It was also my first experience away from my family for any length of time. Even in the dim light of the kerosene lamp in the farmhouse kitchen, I must have looked bad.

At the age of seven years, I didn't know how I looked. I only knew I hadn't felt well all that day. Whatever the cause, I was as sick as anyone that age could be.

I heard my grandmother say, "John, something's wrong with that boy. I can see it from here. He's not acting right and he don't look good to me."

"Well, we best take him to the doctor first thing in the morning," Grandfather motioned with his head.

And that's all I remembered until I woke up in the village doctor's office the next day. I only faintly remember the scene, but I well remember the doctor saying to me, "Son, do you know what homesick is?"

"Yes, I guess so," I answered, in a weak voice. I could just barely hear myself. "It means you're home and you're sick."

"Well, not quite," he replied. "It means you're not home, you miss being home, you miss your mom and dad and your family, and you're sick because you want to be home."

It may have started then, my wanting to be a doctor someday. I had a lingering feeling that the ol' country doctor way back then was a magician when he made that diagnosis and recommended that I be sent home the next day. It may, also, have been a few years later when my family doctor missed diagnosing my acute appendicitis.

I know it had something to do with several mysterious visits another family doctor made to our home over the years. He would go into Mother's bedroom and close the door for a while. A little later, he appeared with another one of my eight siblings. I thought it was some kind of magic for the next three younger than myself. For the last three, I began to realize that something natural was going on.

I, also, recall the strange feeling of my first experience with death. I was no more than a three-year-old myself. A two year old cousin was laid away in his

The Country Doctor

casket at the end of the family living room. In those days, wakes took place at one's own home.

There was something about that distant memory that stayed with me, a need to know more about a mysterious something that happens to a living person. It just didn't seem real or right that death could happen to a young child.

"Johnny-Boy," my grandfather said to me one day. "Look at these. Did you ever see anything like them? Whaddya think they are?"

He handed me a large, white, oblong object. It looked like a very oversized pill measuring a half-inch thick, three quarters of an inch wide, and two inches long. It was a 240-grain, aspirin tablet used for cows and horses. That's twenty-four times the average human adult dose and not just for simple headaches. Animals are smarter than that. Tension headache has no place on their menu of illnesses. The pill was used, instead, for that udder ache of mastitis and the horse's hoof-ache of infection as well as a variety of other animal ills.

The other tablet was an even larger pink pill that measured three quarters of an inch thick, a half-inch wide, and three inches long. Dissolved in a pint of water,

Alive and Well

Pepto-Bismol® treated the large animal's case of indigestion caused by overeating or eating the wrong thing--something shared by animals and human beings alike when both eat like a horse. The result of that treatment was one great big burp. That's all it took to relieve a bovine bellyache.

Administering pills and liquids to an uncooperative animal, one that is not willing to "open wide" and "say ahh," is similar to that in small children. In the case of animals, however, the jaws are pried open by reverse pliers. The pill is then stuffed deep into the throat, well past the voice box, and the patient has no choice but to swallow it. If the medicine is liquid, it is washed in with the help of a small section of garden hose. Words of caution are to keep the hands out of the patient's mouth to avoid amputation and to stand away from the animal's face to avoid a copious throw-up.

In those days my grandparents and my mother lived off the land. The garden was the size of a small field filled with a variety of vegetables that eventually found their way into dozens of jars; pints, quarts, and half-gallons. They ended up on wooden shelves around all sides of the large, cool basement beneath the house, from floor to

The Country Doctor

ceiling and wall to wall. The sight of the basement at the end of harvest time was a picture-perfect rainbow of canned tomatoes, carrots, yellow beans, blueberries, green beans, and grape juice from the little arbor behind the house.

My favorite was the row of half-gallon jugs filled with a rich brown liquid that, when the light of the kerosene lamp reflected off the glass, sparkled like stars on a clear, moonless night. It was birch beer laboriously made from the tree's bark in October while the sap was still in the trunk. It was supposed to be left to ferment for three months until it reached its peak of tasty richness. That shelf was empty after just a few weeks. It was tasty enough by then. The kids just couldn't wait any longer.

But, there was more to living off the land than just cultivating a vegetable garden. Fields and woodlands produced a bountiful supply of fruit that began with wild strawberries in May. In June, huckleberries and blueberries came along. Dewberries followed, with black and red raspberries close behind. The pretty, white, pancake blossoms of the elder ripened into a deep purple to produce a rich, juice-producing berry come August.

Berry season was crowned by the king of them all in August with the ubiquitous, big, black ones, favored by

Alive and Well

the boys who picked them. Much bigger in size than all the others, they filled our pails much quicker.

At the same time, I remember complaining that girls were left out of all that pickin'. It may have been for the same reason fathers worried about them playing in hay mows. Still, we boys would not have traded all those wonderful times in the berry patches and those hours of bare-bottomed swimming in mountain streams near every pickin' patch for what the girls had to do with all that cleaning and canning back in the kitchen.

In the springtime, the dandy, wild dandelion became our salad treat in May. The brew of its blossoms lingered around the calendar as a wine for all seasons.

And, mothers were magicians as well as angels back then. What they could do with the fruit of the land was as mysterious to me as the beautiful flowers that produced the ripened fruit. Mothers could transform it into a wide variety of jellies and jams, pies and biscuits, juices and wines, and all manner of canned things.

It was amazing then, and still is to me, what mothers and nature had wrought for humankind out of which we have questionably benevolent dominion.

The Country Doctor

I remember Grandfather seeming to be out of proportion to his handlebar mustache and to four foot ten inch, one hundred seventy pound Grandmother. So, too, was the energy which he used to keep up with his 150-acre dairy farm.

There was no more comical a pair than they--he a dwarfish little character and she a bouncing, short, and not-so-little gnome. They had crossed the boundary way back then into a fairy tale, social intermarriage.

Sixty years ago, my grandfather worked for his retirement with investments made by the daily deposit of long hours and hard work. He battled the elements then as the few, remaining, small dairy farmers do today. Like them, he fought the federal regulation of milk prices--Big Brother's price-control, a brain child of a lame-brained government.

My grandfather loved the land, and I loved him. I still do as I occasionally reflect in the sweet nostalgia of the quiet darkness of a country kitchen and the flickering shadows of a kerosene lamp.

It's not hard to grow up. Just go from one childhood to another.

Interlude 22

Stillmorpourri

At last count, I've read of at least one hundred ways to relieve hiccups. They range all the way from submerging your head under water for as many minutes as you can hold your breath to experiencing something scary, such as the cost of groceries at the cash register.

I have found the simplest, most effective way is to take as deep a breath as possible and hold it as long as you can. It usually works the first time. If not, try it one or two more times. For me, it has rarely failed to stop the 'cups cold. The bottom line to all these methods is to stop breathing. The only one-hundred-percent guaranteed one is to keep your head submerged under water for longer than you can.

When you have a severe itch that can't wait for a pill to work, use an ice cube for quick, slick relief. It doesn't irritate the skin, spread the rash, or cause infection.

You can make your own soothing, soapless skin cleanser with one-half cup of colloidal oatmeal and one shot glass of baby oil. Don't use water, for it will make the oatmeal rancid.

Chapter 23

Vet For a Day

Humans are the only animals that can laugh at themselves, and they have plenty of reason to.

I just could not turn my friend's dog away when he was brought to me with his nose and mouth sprouting porcupine quills like a cushion littered with pins and needles. It was the third time I'd seen him over the past five years, and it was not a job that Poppy could do himself. It was too painful and took an injection of Pentothal® to put Cooley under before the job could be accomplished. On that occasion, I counted a total of one hundred quills by the time I had finished, and Ol' Cooley would not have allowed that if he were conscious.

"You know, Pop," I said, "each time I see this thing, it amazes me that any dog would get himself into such a fix more than once. It's difficult to believe they don't learn to avoid repeats of such a very painful experience."

"He just doesn't seem to know any better," Cooley's master replied. "I don't understand it myself. He's normally a very smart dog."

Alive and Well

Dottie, the local druggist's wife, called late one night, obviously excited and distraught.

"Dr. John, my cat is having her first litter of kittens and something's wrong. It's been a half hour since the first one and nothing else has happened. She's in pain. The poor thing is struggling as though she can't pass the next one. I'm afraid if something isn't done soon, she could die. Can you do anything?"

"Well, I've never delivered kittens before, but I'll take a look," I agreed, realizing there was no veterinarian closer than twenty-five miles.

Ten minutes later I found myself examining a very weak and moribund feline female. It didn't take long for me to realize that a kitten was caught crosswise in the little mother's birth canal. There was no way it would come out by itself. I inserted a well-lubricated, gloved finger into the vaginal opening and gently manipulated the tiny kitten around. The dead kitten popped out in my hand. Within a few minutes three little ones followed, alive and well, all sniffing and sneezing and beginning to move slowly and cautiously around, looking to their mother for nourishment.

Cloe, a young Labrador retriever and Millie's favorite pet, had been missing for two days.

"It's not like her to do this," Millie related. "She seldom goes very far away from the farm and never fails to show up for food and shelter each day. Have you seen her around your place?"

"No, but I'll keep my eyes and ears open for her."

The next time I heard from Millie, she called me in an obvious state of urgency. "Dr. John, we just found Cloe. She was in a shallow ditch along the road. I think she's been hit by a car. She's still breathing but she's out cold. We can't get her to come around."

"Bring her to the clinic," I said with equal excitement. "I'll see her as soon as you arrive."

We stretched Cloe out on her side on the x-ray table. She lay motionless, breathing regularly and shallow, completely unresponsive. I examined her for any obvious bruises and broken bones. Her chest and abdomen were normal. There were no signs of internal injury. The mucous membranes of her mouth and eyelids were pink and moist.

"Well, I can't find any major injuries, but let's take an x-ray to see if that will tell us anything."

Alive and Well

Cloe's sleek, black body lay stretched out on the table like she belonged there just as much as any person patient in my practice. I first x-rayed her upper half because she was too long from head to foot for one film. The second shot included her lower spine, pelvis, and hind legs. The x-rays came out just right technically and showed no signs of bone or internal injury.

"Millie," I said, "she must have had a hard bump on the head. I believe she's had a concussion. Take her home and watch her closely. Give her as much liquid by mouth as you can, so she doesn't become dehydrated. Keep me posted on her progress.

Over the ensuing days, I remained anxious about Cloe's condition, so I was relieved to hear from Millie three days later. That time, her excitement was equally as intense as before, but considerably more joyful.

"She's coming around, Dr. John! Cloe is awake and getting more alert every day!"

"Wonderful. I'm as happy as you to know she's likely to make it. Sounds like she'll be all right."

Over the next few weeks, Cloe did get slowly and surely better. As I saw her occasionally over the following months, the courageous, young creature recovered and

The Country Doctor

became her own perky self again, except for the way she walked.

Cloe was very active on all four legs and got around as well as her two siblings, but she was unable to run straight. She would head to the right with a certain list, as though her body wanted to move in a circle rather than straight ahead. She managed to overcome the quirk, however, and was able to keep up with the rest as she would trod ahead in a straight direction by shortening the gait of her left front leg and lengthening that of her right.

"You're nothing but a horse doctor," Harley told me one day. At the time, I wasn't sure if it was a compliment or a put-down. I decided it was the former when I glanced up at him to see a lopsided smile play across his usually, very-straight face. I had just sutured a large tear in his horse's face. A motorcycle had collided with the beautiful black stallion several miles down the road from my office, and I was the nearest doctor around.

"That's all right, Harley. After all, horse doctoring isn't necessarily all that different than doctoring people. Complaints are a little more difficult to come by but with careful attention to body language, the diagnosis can be made and the right treatment prescribed. Animal patients get better quicker, too, and are a whole lot less neurotic."

Sore throats had been plaguing the Harringtons for months. Terry and the rest of the family, as well as myself, were getting provoked about seeing one after the other of the three children and the two parents inflicted every couple of weeks.

"What's going on here, Dr. John?" Terry asked, not for the first time. "This is a real bother and a big expense, too. I can't keep paying for all these office visits and medications. There's a lot of missed work and school, too."

"Somebody has to be a carrier," I replied, "and if it's not someone at school or a fellow worker, it must be someone in the family. Let's get to the bottom of it once and for all. Bring the whole family into the office at the same time. I'll do a throat swab on everyone, then treat all of you for the usual ten days and check you all again. By that time, the strep bug should be eradicated from all members of the family."

All five were checked for strep the next day. The mother and ten-year-old Susan were both positive. The entire family was treated and checked again on the day

The Country Doctor

following the last dose of antibiotic. Two weeks later, Terry brought Susan into the office with another sore throat, and once again it checked positive for strep.

"This is awful!" Terry exclaimed. "I'm so disappointed I could scream."

"Well, you scream and I'll cry," was my own frustrated response. "Somehow we've missed something."

The next moment, I heard myself yelling out loud, "Aha! I think I've got it! I know you don't have dogs and cats in your home, but I remember you telling me about Susan's pet parakeet."

"Yes, you're right. We've had her for about a year now. Do you suppose we may have missed the carrier?"

"We'll soon find out," I said. "Take this sterile swab home with you. The next time she opens her beak to talk, chirp, or sing, get some mucus from her throat. I'll check it for strep as soon as possible."

It took only until the following day for Terry to return the swab to me. Within three days we had the answer. The culture was positive. Peggy, the little parakeet, was indeed the carrier. The question of what the family should do was answered for us a week later when Terry called to tell me the bird was found dead in it's cage that very day.

Alive and Well

The problem for Terry's family was solved, at least for the moment.

For me, the question "Is this kind of sore throat a rheumatic strep type?" continues to be a concern. Like the rest of my profession, I felt good about the prospect that rheumatic fever was well on its way to extinction by the end of the late 1970's, at least in the United States and Western Europe. Ten years later, pockets of outbreaks began to again erupt in widely scattered parts of the country. The strep bug is still not dead and gone.

Humans are the only animals that blush;
all others have no need to.

Interlude 23

Acceptance--This Is a Prescription*

*Before taking the prescription, read the seven statements that follow. Then score yourself for each of the five levels.

1. Take the test in a meditative mood and in the quietude of your heart and mind.

2. Make your best judgement of each level of acceptance from 0 to 100%. The top total is 500.

3. Now think of the difference between 500 and your self-determined percent of acceptance as your degree of resignation toward life.

4. Acceptance is active and patient allowance. It is open to hope and positive change.

5. Resignation is passive submission, giving up, without hope for positive change.

6. As simple a thing as it seems, patients tell me that each time they take the test, they become ever closer to 500%.

7. This is a treatment to be used at least once daily for the rest of your life.

  Percent

1. I accept myself, with my imperfections and limitations, and my responsibility for myself.

   _____

2. I accept you, with your imperfections and limitations, and your responsibility for yourself.

   _____

3. I accept my acceptance of myself, and your acceptance of me, with humility and gratitude.

   _____

4. I accept my unacceptance by you and your responsibility for it.

   _____

5. I accept your unacceptance of yourself and your responsibility for it.

   _____

TOTAL

   _____

Chapter 24

A Brain Game

One of the best uses of high-tech medicine may be finding a way to avoid it.

"But my doctor said there's nothing wrong," Frank insisted. "I was told to go home and forget about how I felt. There was nothing serious going on."

"That's just a doctor's way for a quick fix," I replied. "That way there's no need to deal with you any further."

I had known Frank as a casual acquaintance around town for some time, and that was his first medical visit to me for a second opinion. Not too long ago, we had talked on the street corner about the symptoms he had been having for the past six months, so I knew something about his problem.

"Well, all your tests were negative," I said. "We've talked about this before, Frank. It doesn't mean that you're cured or that nothing's wrong. It doesn't mean it's all in your head either. It just means the tests haven't found anything. Perhaps they weren't the right ones, or there aren't any tests that can detect what's wrong or you didn't need any to begin with.

Alive and Well

"In the meantime, you're still tired. Your muscles ache. You sleep without resting. You can't work. You can't do most of the things you used to do."

"So, what am I to do?" Frank asked in obvious resignation.

"Tell me again exactly what has been going on so far, Frank, right from the beginning."

"Okay, I saw the doctor six months ago. We spent ten minutes talking about my symptoms and another five minutes on a physical examination."

"And what tests did you have after that?"

"I had a bunch of blood tests, a chest x-ray, and a cardiogram. Then I had a brain scan and an MRI of my whole spine. After that, there were some special blood tests, more advanced, the doctor said. Later on, I had breathing tests, then allergy studies. I have seen three different specialists, too. I'm thinking some of my tiredness is just from going through all that testing! Can you do anything for me?" he pleaded.

"Well, I've already done ninety percent of what I think you need. We've just spent an hour with your medical history and physical exam. That's what it takes to give you my opinion. That's all I need to decide what you don't have and then to decide what you do have. That's what all those tests were about, to find out what you don't have.

The Country Doctor

"Now, you need to get a hold on what you do have, and that can take a large dose of explanation and reassurance. The final thing you can do for yourself is to accept that you have chronic fatigue."

As we talked more about chronic fatigue and how to handle it, I replayed one of my favorite brain games, "Ninety Percent and Ten":

Ninety percent of all human disease and illness is not necessary.

Ninety percent of all human disease and illness is self-inflicted.

Ninety percent of all human disease and illness is transient and self-healing.

Ninety percent of all human disease and illness does not need professional, health-care providers of any kind.

Ninety percent of all human disease and illness is not seen by health-care providers of any kind.

Ninety percent of money spent on health care goes to somewhere other than to the providers themselves.

Ninety percent of all human disease and illness is psychological or has some significant psychological component.

Ten percent of all human disease and illness is brought to the attention of health-care providers.

Ninety percent of all human disease and illness that comes to the attention of health-care providers can be adequately cared for by primary-care providers, general practitioners, primary-care physicians, internists, obstetricians, gynecologists, occupational and environmental physicians, and emergency room doctors.

Ninety percent of all human disease and illness that comes to the attention of a primary-care provider can be diagnosed and treated by a careful and thorough history, in other words, the patient's primary complaint, a review of all systems of the body, past medical history, and social history.

Ninety percent of the remaining ten percent can be diagnosed and treated with the aid of a complete physical examination.

Ninety percent of the remaining ten percent can be diagnosed and treated with the help of routine testing which includes blood, urine, chest x-ray, and cardiogram.

Ninety percent of the remaining ten percent requires the expertise of a specialist.

Ninety percent of that remaining ten percent requires advanced, high-tech studies.

The ten percent at the bottom requires surgical or invasive treatment of some kind.

As one descends down the list to each succeeding ten percent of the preceding ninety percent, the cost of medical care gradually gets greater.

The Country Doctor

By the time the bottom line is reached, the remaining ten percent accounts for ninety percent of the cost of medical care.

The old, medical model for patient care in country doctor days was ninety percent stop, look, and listen along with an equal amount of intuitive judgment and common sense.

Ten percent of today's managed, health-care model uses the new model of ninety percent tests, x-rays, high-tech studies, organ transplants, and the like.

Some footnotes:

Human disease and illness includes anything from a head cold to life-threatening heart attacks, strokes, and cancer.

Some heart attacks are silent. Some are known only to the individual as minor chest pain, and others are known only at the autopsy table years later.

This essay is loaded with generalities.

These statements are based on a lifetime of medical practice experience and not on one year of experience for a lifetime.

Experience is anyone's best teacher.

Intuitive judgment from anecdotal experience may be as credible as scientific experiment and clinical research focused on controlled studies, both of which may have statistical significance or insignificance.

Emperic-dotal management of illness and disease follows intuitive judgment from anecdotal experience. Emperical refers to treatment with something even though there is no scientific proof of indication and effectiveness. Anecdotal means individual subjective testimony after a treatment for a variable length of time.

There may be some mathematical exaggeration in this essay. The percents may be 89.5 percent to 90.3 percent instead of 90. And, they may be 9.5 percent to 10.3 percent instead of 10.

The previous statements may allow for ninety percent credibility in support of this brain game.

Ninety percent of things not only get better by themselves, they get better by morning.

Interlude 24

Common Sense and Your Health
This Is a Medical IQ Test

What is your:

1. Age?_____
2. Sex? (a bonus question)_____
3. Height?_____
4. Weight?_____ What should it be?_____
5. Blood Pressure?_____ What should it be?_____
6. Pulse Rate?_____ What should it be?_____
7. Blood Sugar?_____ What should it be?_____
8. Cholesterol, Total?_____ What should it be?_____
9. Cholesterol, Good (HDL)?_____ What should it be?_____
10. Cholesterol, Bad (LDL)?_____ What should it be?_____
11. Triglyceride?_____ What should it be?_____
12. Do you exercise one-half hour three or more times a week in addition to your regular work activity? Yes_____ No_____
13. Have you seen a doctor in the past six to twelve months? Yes_____ No_____
14. Have you had routine blood tests in the past six to twelve months? Yes_____ No_____

Alive and Well

If you can't answer the first four questions, you may be dead. If you're not, take 2 Tylenol® tablets, drink lots of water, go to bed, and take the test first thing in the morning.

There are 22 answers to the quiz, each of which will give you approximately five points credit.

If you can answer all questions correctly and check the last three as "yes," you are a medical, self-care genius. For every one not answered or not checked "yes," subtract five points, then grade yourself as genius minus five, ten, fifteen, etc.

You now know what you are. The final question is:
Are you satisfied?
Yes _____ No _____
If you're not, what will you do about it?
_____

_____

Chapter 25

Copter Doctor

Ideas are powerless unless you use them.

Twenty minutes and forty miles away from my valley office in northwestern Pennsylvania I began to manipulate my whirlybird to prepare for landing. Cedarville, one of my three satellite offices, was a few miles away and there was an emergency waiting for me.

My descent was always a multi-jockey event as if I were driving three race horses, all at the same time and from one saddle. It demanded that kind of attention for me to get out of the air and onto the ground until I learned to fly by the seat of my pants, two arms, two legs, a lot of head, and a little luck!

My right hand held the stick that moved the ship's nose up, down, right, or left. My left hand gripped the power stick which raised and lowered the copter from ground to hover. At the same time, my two feet operated the pedals that moved the rudders. Now and then, I adjusted the throttle with my right hand to help maintain speed and de-ice the engine.

Alive and Well

I recalled again, for the nth time, my instructor's urgent voice, "Watch your forward speed! You're too slow! You're losing altitude! De-ice the engine or you'll stall out! That's better. Now sight your landing target far enough ahead. You want to come in just above the hover point. Right on!" Marty would shout.

Those were the early days of my helicopter flight training and I had listened to many such commands from Marty.

"Marty," I would respond. "Do you realize how difficult this is for me? I am a slow learner when it comes to using both hands and feet and one head all at the same time."

I have never been all that left-brained. Things mathematical and mechanical don't come to me with the snap of a switch. The fact that I bought the helicopter before I knew how to fly it had never been a concern in my own mind, but Sam, my accountant, reminded me of the foolishness of it more than a few times over the next couple of years.

"You've got the aircraft," Marty would say, and that meant that I was then the pilot. My head would go into another spin with hands and feet moving up and down and back and forth. The copter would turn and roll a few

The Country Doctor

times and then level off. As we went along, I knew Marty wondered whether I would ever solo that fluttering contraption. And, so did I.

I began to make occasional secret trips to the airstrip that was just ten minutes from my office. It had to be in secret, for it went strongly against some very firm rules for a student to be in the cockpit with the engine running without an instructor. Only when Marty felt confident would I solo.

I was eager for that. I wanted to show Marty I wasn't as slow a learner as we both thought. My greatest fear was that I might flip over and catch the main prop on the ground. In a split second that would mean flip-flopping all over the place like a pair of wet socks in a clothes dryer trying to find which end was up. That fear eventually left me, but the thought never did.

One day I stood near the edge of the landing strip of the small airfield waiting for Marty to come in with my copter from the west. Looking up, I saw a spectacularly ominous cloud cover extending across the vault of the sky from one end to the other. It was rolling rapidly in my direction, and I knew that, in the face of the storm, Marty would not be coming.

Alive and Well

As the threat passed, I stayed on to watch a group of sky divers practice their colorful and breathtaking exercises. A large circle lay out on the ground nearby. It was covered with small pebbles and concaved slightly upward. That was the target the sky divers aimed for as they practiced what, in my opinion, was a very courageous art.

I never forgot the sky diver's target. Marty used it as a landing pad for the copter one day. Because the target was concave, the copter tilted back just enough to catch the tail prop on the pebbles and knock it a little out of whack. The prop had to be replaced to the tune of one thousand dollars. I was glad he did it and paid for it and not I. It was a great way to teach me a lesson.

"So, today we will begin practicing stalls," Marty related, as I lifted the copter off the ground to a height of about 50 feet. I hovered for an instant, tilted the main prop forward, increased the power, and fluttered away into a clear, cool October sky.

Two thousand feet into the air, Marty said, "Okay. Let's see you do it."

The Country Doctor

We flew straight on for a few miles as Marty owled his head around looking for a suitable landmark. "See that silo down there? That's our target. Get ready."

"Marty, I can't even see the barn. And where's the ground?" In truth, I did see the silo. It looked like the head of a small straight pin.

"Keep your eye on it. You'll soon see it," insisted Marty, whereupon he cut the engine and the copter obliged by promptly dropping like a huge rock into a quiet pool of water. It was still possible to guide the copter as it dropped by using a forward/backward manipulation of the stick, which moved the main prop back and forth as it sliced through the air. The barn and silo were quickly within several hundred feet and the ground was looking very close!

"Switch the engine on!" Marty demanded.

"I'll be happy to!" I shouted.

Another fear was overcome as I again learned the importance of turning on the power before the ship got too close to the ground. "Too close" meant there was not enough air and distance to recover lift.

Each time I practiced stalls, I realized the difference between fixed-wing plane and copter stalls. The momentum of a fixed-wing plane was gradually upward with steadily decreasing power until the engine conked out and the plane fell downward. My heart was in my mouth at that point of sudden change.

With the copter, the sensation was different. As the copter plummeted, I felt my heart at the lower end of my anatomy. The first time I had felt like that was when the ski lift suddenly left the top to descend the snowless slopes of Whiteface Mountain during a summer sightseeing trip. And, the feeling is the same, an adrenalin high, sensual but not orgasmic.

Gradually, stall outs became freer and easier, and I tipped my hat to myself and to the good earth two thousand feet below me each time I flapped along at one hundred miles an hour. I had to keep reminding myself how quickly I could fail and fall. It takes an immense amount of concentration to keep that high-tech top in the air.

I developed a great admiration for clouds and birds and their ease for staying in the air during my copter training. At that moment, however, I was busy looking out through the floor window to my left, and down to the ground, for the clinic building to come into view.

The Country Doctor

Whirling lights were flashing about in all directions, and I wondered what kind of emergency was awaiting me. The Cedarville ambulance with its full crew was parked in the street nearby along with the local fire truck and several dozen spectators. It was plain to see they were expecting me.

As soon as the prop stopped rotating, I shoved the door open and yelled, "What do you have, Joe?"

Joe, one of the local, very capable Emergency Medical Technicians, came racing toward me. "It's the Brad Keefer baby, Doc," he said, breathlessly. "The firemen just pulled him from a trailer fire! He's unconscious from smoke inhalation! He's got a pulse but no breathing!"

"Get him in the copter. Keep him on oxygen," I added. "Make room for his father." Mentally, I was rapidly calculating, weighing the facts. An Enstrom F-28 helicopter has a very small cockpit. It is equipped with two seats and can carry three passengers with a combined weight of about five hundred pounds. Could I transport the baby and father while Joe administered oxygen? I wasn't certain.

It was 1977. My helicopter enabled me to reach patients in outlying rural areas that needed my kind of help. By linking satellite clinics together with helicopter and radio and hiring physician's assistants to staff the clinics, I had succeeded in lightening the heavy patient load in my valley office and in accommodating the people who needed emergency and regular medical care in rural communities.

I decided that the Keefer baby's needs were far greater than my concerns regarding weight recommendations. Within minutes, the four of us were squeezed in and the door was closed. I revved the engine and started the prop. The engine was hot and ready to go, but our ascent was slow and laborious. I coaxed the throttle and gritted my teeth. A quick and silent prayer went up with us as I swung her around, due west, and moved out.

Along the way, the baby's heart stopped beating. We had several anxious moments as Joe did CPR. Back then, cardiopulmonary resuscitation was in its infancy as a standard practice. Reviving victims of drowning, electric shock, or other catastrophes, including strokes or heart attacks, had always been part of an art practiced only by medical professionals. Fortunately for the Keefer child, Joe, a first-rate technician, and others like him, were becoming important members of the health-care team.

The Country Doctor

Evolving out of Red Cross and scout first-aid programs and turning into professional EMT's and Paramedics, they are often the first responders to appear on the scene of immediate need. They can make the difference between life and death.

Once in the air, I went on the radio with the State Police. It was my only means of communicating with the hospital emergency room.

"This is Copter Doctor," I shouted over the noise of the rotors. "Helicopter 379 CD60. Come in, please. Over."

"This is State Police Radio PA 37 E10," a voice said in quick response. "We read you, Copter Doctor. What's the problem? Over."

"I have a year-old child with smoke inhalation," I replied. "Unconscious, not breathing. EMT CPR is sustaining him. I am ten minutes from the hospital. Over."

"What's your MO? Over."

"Alert the emergency room. Have their receiving team on the sidewalk in about eight minutes. Over and out."

"Roger, Copter Doctor. Over and out."

Alive and Well

The universal emergency call number, 911, was many years in the future. Back in 1977, it took at least several phone calls and many precious minutes to summon help. Today, a single quick call handles the problem and saves many lives each year in those most critical first few minutes of an emergency situation.

We did a pretty good job back then when the specialized hospital trauma units were unborn and unconceived. EMT's, paramedics, community ambulance services, and ordinary emergency room departments of small community hospitals were the saviors of human lives.

The hospital heliport was not in the picture in those days either, so the street next to the emergency room entrance was cleared for our landing by the Linden City police. The fire company was also there in case of trouble, something I preferred not to think about.

We were about two thousand feet in the air when my vantage point put me in visual contact with the hospital. We were close enough for direct contact with the hospital radio.

The Country Doctor

"This is Copter Doctor 379 CD60," I said. "I'll be on the street in less than a minute. The child needs a ventilator immediately."

"Okay, doctor," a nurse quickly responded. "We're ready for him."

As the prop stopped and the receiving team took over, I became aware of the tension in my muscles. The unconscious baby disappeared from my sight, and I knew that he had a good chance for survival because of the speed of the copter. The entire trip, from ground zero some forty miles away to the street in front of the emergency room, had taken fifteen minutes. Any other means of transportation would have required a minimum of an hour.

As my own heart rate returned to normal, I gave the copter an appreciative pat on the bubble. Not once had it complained about the overload. And, I promised to never again ignore its weight limit. At least, not right away.

Old pilots never die; they just fly away.

Interlude 25

Life Is A Risk

If you were not alive, there would be no risk of dying. Since you are, there is opportunity for living to the fullest.

Being alive also means threat of disease and death. Uncontrollable threats may have to do with your sex, age, heredity, and, to some extent, where you live in the world.

Controllable threats include your weight, blood pressure, cholesterol, triglycerides, sugar, uric acid, excessive emotional stress, inadequate physical activity, abuse of food, alcohol, drugs, tobacco, television or caffeine, and a negative mental attitude.

A quick run-down of controllable and uncontrollable threats to living can give all of us a very positive edge with which to optimize the quality of our lives. Deal with those over which you have control. Accept, without resignation, those that you cannot.

Chapter 26

Different Strokes for Different Folks

Women are stronger than men because they accept their weaknesses with greater confidence.

In the average doctor's office, women outnumber men about nine to one. I've decided it's because they are generally more accepting when something is wrong and are more willing to do something about it. They are less fearful of facing their physical and emotional adversities. That's why women outlive men by five years or more. The majority of people in the United States over one hundred years of age are female. They are the stronger sex as well as the smarter, especially when it comes to taking care of their physical and mental health. Of course, most men think otherwise.

Mattie was no exception. At the age of eighty-seven, she was taking care of herself in her own special way. I had come to know of her long before we actually met. Her daughter and son-in-law had been regular patients for several years, and Gary described her to me on several occasions during his own office visits.

Alive and Well

"My wife's mother lives with us, Doc," he related. "She's been acting very strange for some time and it's getting worse."

"What do you mean, strange?" I asked.

"Well, she stays in her room all the time. She won't come out except to go to the bathroom two or three times a day. We have to take food to her, and she won't take a bath or change her clothes for months at a time. I wish you would see her."

For an instant, my nasal passages dilated with olfactory memory traces of other such patients over the years. Certain smells are permanently stored in one's memory bank and Gary's description of Mattie's room flipped the pages of my mind on to some especially malodorous ones.

"She also sees and hears things that aren't really there," Gary continued. "She talks to people outside her window and in her clothes closet. She carries on conversations as if someone were in the room with her.

"She won't come to the office," Gary said emphatically. "She hasn't been out of the house for fifteen years and hasn't seen a doctor since she was sick with pneumonia twenty-five years ago."

I was becoming increasingly more interested in Mattie. "If she absolutely won't come to the office, I'll see her the next time I make my house call rounds."

The Country Doctor

I sensed the winds of change as my Chunker and I wound our way into the edge of the woodlands at the outskirts of Susquehoning.

There is a spiciness to the cool breezes of late August that is as tasty as it is fragrant. Nature's sounds are more subdued after the exuberance of spring's and summer's maturation.

Plant life demonstrates the greatest change as tree and bush and grass begin their transformation from natural green to kaleidoscopic flaming foliage. Grasses turn to a hibernating, straw-brownish tan. The dainty little pale blue leaves of huckleberry bushes turn to an intense bright purple and hip-deep, hay-scented fern spotlight the forest floor with bronze and gold.

The ultimate miracle is the vision of a single, sugar maple tree captured for a moment in time when its still-full canopy glows with splashes of nearly all colors of the rainbow--red, orange, yellow, leftover green, and even the hues of blue and lavender.

No one and nothing can handle colors like Mother Nature and her magic wand. The symphony of autumn is more than sight and sound or fragrance and taste. It is a feeling inside the mind and deep within the body. It is the antithesis of spring's lighthearted and exciting growth. It is a quiet withdrawal into my spiritual self where I connect with my own wholeness and that of all things and all creatures great and small in this heaven on earth.

All too soon, I returned to the reality of the moment just in time to spot the McFarland's small, two-bedroom dwelling on a steep hillside at the very edge of town.

I was intrigued when I entered the basement floor level after rapping at the door several times without getting a response. The living-type room was dark and cluttered with an excessive amount of furnishings. It was apparent that the room was used for storage and not for living. The musty smell, the dampness, and the darkness were not at all inviting. I dodged a curtain of cobwebs and looked furtively one way and then another, watching for flying things over my head and crawling things under my feet. Encountering none, I called out, "Hello, is anybody home?"

A muffled voice came to me from a stairway leading up to the second floor, the living quarters for Mattie, her daughter Eloise, and Gary. The voice invited me up, and I was directed to a small bedroom in the back corner of the house. The intensely unpleasant odor of unwashed bedding and clothing overloaded my senses.

The entire room was a shambles. I finally recognized what turned out to be Mattie's diminutive, frail body mixed up in the disheveled mass of sheets and blankets.

The Country Doctor

Her hair was an uncombed, unwashed mess. Not only had she not bathed for some time, I observed smatterings of feces on the bedding.

It took some deep breath holding and a quick examination to check Mattie's blood pressure and pulse and to listen to her heart. Despite her lack of good hygiene, my intuition was keen enough to know that the poor, abandoned old soul was physically all right. However, she had been allowed to degenerate into a badly neglected, eighty seven year old "non-person" who was suffering from mental illness, senility, or Alzheimer's disease. It would be a trick to figure out which.

Mattie was not very talkative and had no complaints. I was able to engage her attention by asking her about herself and getting occasional answers during the course of our visits over the following months. Answers to my questions about her physical health were normal and reasonable enough. She felt well, despite her poor eating and her dismal unhygienic condition. Her fingers and toenails were badly in need of cleaning and trimming. Her body was equally in need of bathing.

"Mattie," I implored after several visits. "Are you ready to let me trim your nails? I promise you it won't hurt. I really believe you will feel much better afterwards."

Alive and Well

She gave me her permission, and when the task had been completed, Mattie beamed from ear to ear. She did, indeed, feel and look better.

As our relationship progressed, Mattie became trusting enough to introduce me to her imaginary friends. They turned out to be pretty nondescript and varied from one or two men and two or three women with whom she talked. They were not always there at the same time.

"What do your friends want?" I asked Mattie on a number of occasions. "What do they say to you?"

"Oh, we just chat about anything and everything. They are my friends," she replied in a matter-of-fact way. "I've known them for a long time. I'm glad they visit with me like they do."

For myself, I found it easy enough to believe in Mattie's imaginary friends. She made them sound so real. At times, I was tempted to see and talk with them myself. I accepted them as a necessary part of Mattie's life. I knew better than to deny their existence. It would have been the quickest way to lose her confidence. They were real enough for her, and she was certainly better off with them than with the "real" people in her household.

After I had seen Mattie several times, Gary asked, "Whaddya think, Doc? Does she have Alzheimer's disease?"

The Country Doctor

"No, she doesn't, Gary," I responded, "and I'm not sure what that really is. It seems to be a loosely-used, diagnostic label these days, both by people in general and the medical profession. Most of the time what is now casually called Alzheimer's disease is, in effect, the senility of not so many years ago. It's been said that only about ten percent of such cases are true Alzheimer's disease victims, and Mattie is not one of them. It can be proven with a careful history, physical examination, and blood tests.

"Nor, do I think she has any serious mental illness," I added. "She is no more psychotic than most people I know. She may have a bit of senility, but so do many individuals her age. Forgetfulness is all right. Memories can come and go for any of us. For older people, it can even be a blessing. It helps lighten their feelings of sadness and abandonment. It allows them to forget when relatives are gone and friends never come.

"Mattie hasn't been out of the house for fifteen years, not because she is unable to leave, but because she doesn't want to leave. She has no reason to come out of her room.

"Also, I don't believe she's hallucinating. She merely embellishes her life with pleasant company. After all, if healthy little children can do it, why not Mattie? It's her way of widening her world beyond the narrow confines of her room and this house. That way she's not so alone.

"Gary, Mattie doesn't need a lot of testing or any particular medication but she does need to be treated like a person. She needs someone with whom she can visit. She's lonely and she's human. And, she could use some assistance with her daily living. If you and your wife can't provide it, let's call the Home Health Agency to come in.

"The same thing happens in nursing homes," I added. "Mental and physical deterioration occurs for the old folks because of an absence of familiar faces and voices. They need stimulating conversation to give them a reason to be up and moving, to be thinking and talking, to maintain a recollection of the past, contact with the present, and hope for the future.

"These are needs that are a common denominator for all of us, including the elderly and home-bound. A social life is as important as food, medicine, and physical care requirements."

Why isn't a hysterectomy a hersterectomy?

Interlude 26

A Patch For A Pill

In recent years, a new way of taking medicine has come onto the medical scene. In addition to liquids, pills, and capsules that are taken by mouth, rectum, nose, lungs, and injection, certain medications can be absorbed through the skin from a patch. The patch is applied to an area of the skin which is flat, where it will not shift loose with body movements.

The first of these was the nitroglycerin patch for angina or chest pain due to coronary heart disease. This method, which takes the place of tablets dissolved under the tongue or swallowed into the stomach, requires that the patch be changed daily.

Another is the so-called "anti-age" patch for women. It allows female hormones to be absorbed into the bloodstream to treat hot flashes, night sweats, and the vaginal dryness of menopause. The patch takes the place of tablets by mouth and periodic injection and is changed twice a week.

Alive and Well

A third is Transderm Scope® which releases scopolamine into the system to treat the nausea and vomiting of motion sickness.

A further example is the nicotine patch, changed daily, which aids moderate to heavy smokers in breaking the tobacco habit.

The latest patch is Duragesic® for pain. It can remain an active pain reliever for up to three days.

Patch medications have become increasingly more accepted by both doctors and patients. The amount of medicine that gets into the system can be controlled more effectively, and there is no upset to the stomach.

Because patches come in different strengths, and because they may not be the best choice for everyone, it is necessary for your doctor to help determine the best method and dose for you.

Look for more different kinds of medications to become available in patch form as time goes by.

Chapter 27

Home Baked Bread

The best treatment for birth and death is to enjoy the interval.

After many years of general practice, I've learned that a lot of people really do know what's best for them. I didn't always feel that way, especially during my first few years out of medical school and hospital training. It was not long, however, before I began to learn, and continue to relearn, that a patient can often be his or her own best caretaker. I am content just to be around to help--to cure sometimes, to relieve more often, to comfort always.

As I stomped across the frigid porch of the Gordons' old farm house, Cora met me at the door. "Quick, come on in out of the cold before you freeze to death!"

I was happy enough to oblige since the snow outside was over a foot deep and the temperature measured twenty degrees below zero.

"You didn't have to come out here on a day like this!" Henry exclaimed.

"Well, you were on my house-call list for today along with a dozen others, and I know how hard it is for both of you to get out, even on a good day," I remarked.

Cora was one of my favorite ol' folk patients. She had a multitude of health problems: obesity, arthritis, diabetes, high blood pressure, heart palpitations, poor circulation, cancer of the bowel and pelvis, chronic ingrown toenails, osteoporosis of the bone, emphysema, an underactive thyroid, blockage of the neck arteries, high cholesterol, cataracts, and hemorrhoids. And that was all in one eighty year old body, all at the same time. She had her share of occasional colds and viruses as well.

In addition to the diseases I was able to identify, there were many other symptoms so general that neither she nor I could put labels on them. And, Cora was not a hypochondriac. She complained a lot, because her complaints were real.

It was a tremendous chore for Cora to live with her physical infirmities, and it was a challenge for me to try to treat such a vast array of symptoms and conditions. We both tried. A change in diet for this, exercise for that, a pill for this, a syrup for something else. There was at least one treatment for each of her maladies. It was no surprise to me that Cora periodically skipped one or two. She would either forget a medication or confuse its timing.

The Country Doctor

Occasionally, she felt she was having side effects from some of her medications. During each visit, I carefully reviewed both Cora's and Henry's pills and capsules. Some had been prescribed by myself, others by several specialists.

Henry would take me to three different places in the house where his medications were stored. First was the kitchen counter top, where there were three of his current medications, or so he thought. Then, we would check the bathroom, where three other prescriptions were placed on the left side of the first shelf. He had positioned them so he would take them at just the right time. Since he could not read the labels, he relied on the placement of the bottles--one on the first shelf, one on the left, and so on. I wondered how he was able to, despite his poor vision, put them in their particular locations in the first place.

On the middle and upper shelves were an array of other bottles, eight all told. Three of them were partially filled with the same medications found in the kitchen and on the lower shelf of the cabinet on the left. Two of bottles were without labels. Four others had been outdated, discontinued, or replaced by new prescriptions. They had been prescribed by a total of five different doctors, two of whom Henry hadn't seen for over five years. The fifth doctor had died four years earlier.

Alive and Well

On the other side of the bathroom another batch of bottles was stored on another counter top. Some of those were Henry's and some were Cora's. The whole bunch was a conglomeration of duplicated, outdated, or unlabeled prescriptions.

My search-and-find review was clinched with the discovery of a half-dozen empty bottles and another loaded with pills that had been prescribed thirteen years earlier by another physician who had long since passed away.

There were times when Cora simply became fed up. "I have no time for anything else!" she would exclaim. "It takes me some doin' to take in any food and drink."

I'd take that complaint with a chuckle and a grain of salt since, with her ongoing widespread obesity, she was in no danger of fading away.

That day was one of Cora's fed-up days.

"I've stopped all my medicines," she announced. "The only thing I take now and then is Tylenol®. I don't miss any of it. I think I might even feel better."

"Well, I won't disagree with you, Cora. I'm here today for a blood sample to check your sugar and potassium level."

"I do want to know how I'm doing without all that medicine," she admitted with a smile. "And, I need my toenails trimmed again. It's not that they're long. They just grow into my skin. That's not good for my feet because of my sugar, you know. Besides, it hurts and I have trouble walking without hurting myself."

"Okay, after I get your blood samples."

I always felt lucky to get samples of blood from Cora's veins. Her weight and age made it tricky, and I was not always confident of success.

As I knelt on the floor, trimming one toenail after another, clippings flying all over the room, I listened again to Cora's complaints of wrist pain, itchy eyelids, weak bladder, rectal soreness, wobbly legs, lightheadedness, leg cramps at night, cold feet, earache, flashing lights, and brittle fingernails. She was always in good voice, rambling on and on like the elementary school teacher she was thirty years before.

"Will you stay and have some fresh baked bread and coffee?" Cora asked as I clipped the last toenail down to a nice, neat trim.

From the moment I had stepped into the house a half hour earlier, I had smelled the mouth-watering aroma. I had been hoping she would ask.

"The only thing my old body would let me do today was to bake two loaves of bread, one for us and one for you."

Alive and Well

"I don't see how I can refuse," said my mouth, already savoring the taste.

When I later left that indomitable couple, I sandwiched my loaf of bread under my arm, between my black bag and nail trimming equipment, and, once again marveled. Both Cora and Henry were miracles of survival. I suspect that was due to their genes and grit, and not to anything I was doing.

Smile with a gentle heart.

Interlude 27

Common Sense and Nutrition

Some Highlights

1. A healthful diet has three commonsense qualities: variety, moderation, and balance.
2. Common sense denominators for any diet are low fat, low sugar, and low salt.
3. A healthful diet has a balance of the five food groups:

   a. Breads, cereals, rice, pasta
   b. Vegetables
   c. Fruits
   d. Milk and dairy products.
   e. Meat, poultry, fish, beans, eggs, nuts

4. You can have a healthful diet wherever you eat: home, work, party, guest dinner, restaurant, cafeteria--everywhere and anywhere.
5. You can have a healthful diet whether you eat quickly or slowly and whether you eat day or night.

Alive and Well

6. You can overeat whether you eat quickly or slowly. It takes only a few minutes to eat and drink a lot more calories than you need.
7. Good nutrition, with foods that provide variety, balance, and taste, need not be expensive.
8. The way you cook can help; concentrate on stir-frying, broiling, and microwaving.
9. Water and other low-calorie liquids can curb your appetite and dilute your food intake. Drink reasonable amounts before and during your meal. Keep in mind that water has weight, too; a pint is a pound the world around and around your middle as well.
10. Beware of alcoholic drinks, too much and too long before eating; they can stimulate your appetite and dull your senses to how much you eat.

Chapter 28

Rip's Van Wrinkle

Sleep is the best possible cure for insomnia.

The vision of Washington Irving's *Rip Van Winkle* came to mind as my Chunker and I found our way to Myron's house in the deep woods of Laurel County.

He was another of those "phantom" patients. I occasionally heard about him from his wife, a regular patient over the years. Elsie had talked about Myron for a few minutes each time during her own visits. The story was a familiar one.

"Doc, there ain't no way he'll come to you. He hasn't seen a doctor for ten years. He's getting steady worse. Tired all the time; sleeps a lot. I have to feed him almost e'r'thing he eats and drinks. If it warnt fer me, he would jus' fade away. He won't even go to the bathroom without me a-hounding him and a-helpin' him. It's all a body can do to clean up after him when I don't sit 'im on the pot quick enough. Lord, I dunno what t' do! Ain't fittin' to be sleeping all the time. I'm 'bout at the end of my rope."

"Now, now, Elsie," I said, as I held her rough, work-worn hands in mine. "You know I'll be glad to see him."

Alive and Well

"I reckon he'll never come in though," she responded as she slowly recovered her composure. "You'll have to come out, or he'll never get any help."

"Look for me this coming Wednesday when I make my regular house-call rounds," I remarked, as I escorted her to the reception room.

I have never been certain where the term "rounds" originated, though doctors use the expression routinely. Of course, it refers to the doctor's visits to his patients, whether they be in a hospital, a nursing home, or on house calls. Such itineraries are not really round. They can be square, triangular, trapezoid, or any other geometrical configuration, depending on how long the doctor stays at the bedside. My house calls are an interesting combination of them all. So I see Wednesday as the day of my house-call circuit, an appropriate description, since I always end up at the place from where I started, regardless of directions and miles.

Myron was very well reclined on his lazyman's chair when I entered the room. In fact, with his feet propped up on a foot stool, he was almost horizontal. He lay toward one side, curled up like an unborn baby in his mother's womb, sound asleep and motionless. Without waking him, I examined him as best I could from head to foot. I

The Country Doctor

found his eyes by peering into what I thought was his face. I then worked up from the end of his twenty-year-long, gray, shaggy beard toward what seemed to be his hair that dropped down from what must have been the top of his head. I felt like a veterinarian trying to diagnose my patient's problem without knowing the symptoms or medical history. It would not be the last time my intuition was going to play a big part in my attention to old Rip. Nor would I ever have the help of blood tests and x-rays to make sense of his problem. It would have taken an ambulance and stretcher to get him from that chair to a hospital.

It was not the first time I had to rely exclusively on the contents of my black bag and my head to diagnose and treat a patient in the office or at home. I reminded myself, once again, that ninety percent of all infirmities can be diagnosed and treated after a thorough medical history and physical examination. That is true in the country as well as the city, in the home and office as well as the hospital. Costly blood tests, x-rays, special studies, and specialist care are grossly over utilized in today's medical care scene.

Ah, what a change, I thought. Forty years ago I was able to make the majority of diagnoses with a blood pressure cuff, a stethoscope, and an otoscope. I could treat most of the ailments I encountered with one of the several dozen bottles of pills and liquids in my well-stocked bag. The practitioners of long ago and far away had a great big supply of common sense and compassion to complement that wonderful ol' black bag.

On my way back to the office, the beautiful scenery and the motion of my Chunker on the curves and hills and in the valleys of mountain country roads lulled me into my own case of Rip van Winkle's syndrome. I reflected on the country's medical care scene and the systems that are such a large part of its structure. Once again I was struck by the system's rigid and conventional tradition despite high technology and dramatic advances.

We, in the system and many outside the system, give health-care professionals all the credit for bringing a halt to a variety of infectious diseases which ran rampant over the lives of people a hundred years ago. There are those of us who boast, "Just look at what we've done to prolong life! Aren't we wonderful?"

But, what about the quality of that life? What about giving credit to the sanitary engineers and the water works people who have provided us with clean, comfortable living conditions? Are they not the ones who have made the biggest difference?

In truth, the medical system, of which I am part, deals with about 10 percent of the action. We provide the

The Country Doctor

icing on the care cake to prolong life. Much of what we do adds to life's quantity with little regard for its quality.

Where are we, then, at the beginning of the twenty-first century? What is going on here compared to one hundred years ago? What has happened in between, and what should we look for some fifty more years down the road? Will family doctoring have any answers? Will it have a place?

Unlike Rip van Winkle, Myron did not wake up at the end of twenty years. After a three-year struggle, Elsie could no longer care for him at home. He spent several months in a nursing home, then simply faded away. His cause of death was never known for sure.

Rip van Winkle was able to sleep for twenty years because his neighbors didn't have a radio.

Interlude 28

To Sleep Or Not To Sleep

If you decide you truly have insomnia, try the following Common sense rules for self-treatment:

1. Don't let it frustrate you; that only makes it worse.
2. Don't nap during the evening.
3. Work out a pre-sleep ritual; psych yourself toward bedtime and sleep.
4. Don't go to bed too early.
5. Don't drink alcoholic and stimulating beverages near bedtime or during the night.
6. Engage in some vigorous evening exercise for about a half hour.*
7. Don't take sleep medications for more than ten days.
8. Go to bed with pleasant thoughts and quiet, relaxing music.
9. Have a comfortable warm bed, but a cool room.
10. Don't stay in bed for more than a half hour if you're unable to relax. Remember that bedtime is for physical rest as well as sleep. You don't need to be sound asleep the entire time.

* Sexual intimacy can help to satisfy suggestion #6. There is no limit to the length of time. Also, it fits well with suggestions #8 and #9.

Chapter 29

Myai

You can say a mouthful with your eyes.

There is a place for country doctoring even in the mountains of Central Africa, and I was quick to feel at home in Dembi Dollo in the southwestern corner of Ethiopia.

I relearned there that being human is to share in that which is common the world over, pain and suffering, injury and disease. Sometimes there is cure, often relief, and always comfort. The denominator is no different whether the numerator is in the city, slum, or rural countryside.

There is a language that is universal, common to all humankind and understood just as well as the spoken word. It is spoken by the way one stands and walks. It is accentuated by the waving of hands and open arms, underscored by the tone of voice, parenthesized with a smile, and culminated with the eyes. It is understood by way of one's body, mind, and heart.

Nahab spoke to me with his eyes as he lay flat on his back, unable to move anything below his neck. Three

Alive and Well

weeks before I had arrived, he had been high in a tree, trying to retrieve a large bolus of honey from a bee's nest. He fell onto his head, severing his spinal cord, never to walk again.

There was, also, four year old Hobby who stood on a pair of crutches I had fashioned from the branches of a tree. He had fallen from that same tree a week before, fracturing his right thigh, and had been waiting for me to arrive. It was the first pair of crutches I had ever made. They looked crude and strange, but they worked. He was able to stand and hobble about without too much difficulty. His expression of thanks was a great big smile as broad as his face. There was no misunderstanding that.

Iaea spoke to me with second degree burns over fifty percent of her very small, two year old body. The single-room, thatched huts that most of the natives lived in were fueled for cooking by an open fire in the center. It was easy enough for young children to fall into them, suffering first to third degree burns from small parts to the entire body.

I heard Geia speak to me loud and clear with multiple tropical ulcers on his legs from feet to hips. Small cuts, scrapes, and insect bites were quick to become infected in the very unsanitary world of the African back country. The end point was eroding cavities

The Country Doctor

filled with foul purulence that burrowed ever deeper into and underneath the skin. Those tragic souls spoke most often with quiet acceptance. When my eyes met theirs it was plain to hear their pleas for help.

The land spoke a language of its own. In the rainy season, the luxurious foliage that covered the hills and filled the valleys of the escarpment spoke with the music of rich tropical green. It was a voice that was echoed by an intensely blue sky that stretched over a broad vista of the land which, in turn, was accentuated by billowing marshmallow-white clouds. I decided there are no bigger, better, or higher rainbows in the world than there. During the rainy season, frequent tropical storms quickly came and went. Near the end of the day, the western sun often projected its light into the vaporous eastern sky to give birth to that eternal multi-colored promise. The violet band on the underside was just as distinct as the red on top.

Groups of natives spoke with the language of work as they stood around a large tree that was blown down by the winds of the last thunder shower. Fallen trees were utilized down to the smallest twig. Small branches were bundled and tied to be used as fuel. Larger ones became a part of huts and other necessary buildings. The tree's trunk, up to four feet in diameter was placed on the ground in ten-foot lengths. Pairs of natives powered a

Alive and Well

large, cross-cut saw, horizontal fashion, and sliced the entire log into boards one-inch thick. It took many pairs of natives to complete the job.

Men and women alike spoke the language of affection as they met on the dirt streets of Dembi Dollo and in their huts and churches. They approached each other with open arms and added a snug, little hug. Alternately, they kissed each other on the forehead, each cheek, the tip of the nose and chin, and then, lightly on the lips. Smiles and a final squeeze ended the greeting which was used for goodbyes as well.

The small, thirty-five-bed hospital on the mission grounds served the town and surrounding countryside. It consisted of a main building for inpatients and a number of tiny clinic and storage buildings, all connected by cement walks that were edged on each side with corn of the season. The corn grew as high as a full-grown, African elephant's eye by harvest time, for there was great fertility in the soil.

Grass grew exuberantly around the tuberculosis and leprosy clinics. It was neatly mowed by several pet goats. What the goat mowers missed was fine-tune trimmed by young native boys with small hand sickles.

The Country Doctor

And, I remember Myai. She was the prettiest of the scenery and spoke the sweetest language simply by her general demeanor.

It took no time at all for me to like her. First sight was sufficient for me to know she was different from the other female natives. Definitely one of a kind. There was a certain poise about her, and she walked with a casual, lilting gait. She possessed a self-confident bearing and had a beautiful smile to match.

Myai's skin was a light tan, smooth as a tender young child's, though I knew her to be in her early twenties. She was unweathered and wrinkle free, unlike most of the other women. She was a pure and simple beauty--virginal in more than a sexual way--unspoiled by the hand of the white man and respected by her own countrypeople.

Myai exuded wholesomeness, health, and an unassuming childlike naturalness by the way she walked and talked and otherwise expressed herself with her body language. She fulfilled all the criteria of what is universally attractive in a young woman without the need or the greed of erotic fantasy. My own attraction to her was one of sincere appreciation.

We learned to communicate with each other in simple ways, our eyes, our smiles, and an occasional light touch. Soft sounds and a variety of body movements

Alive and Well

helped. Our language transcended the gap of generation, race, time, and place. Our understanding of each other was a simple knowing, a sincere and unconditional fondness for each other.

It was natural for Myai and I to befriend each other. While I would be on my way to and from the hospital each day, she would be going in the opposite direction to and from the clinic where she worked. Our meeting was always unplanned; it just happened.

In the morning, it was a simple passing by each other, since we were both intent on our destinations for the day. At the end of the day, time was more casual. We would sit on a fallen tree log and visit briefly, less than a half hour each time. They were quiet visits, for we knew very little of each other's verbal language. The only Amharic I had learned consisted of simple words and phrases that had to do with symptoms, disease, and medicine. But, the absence of words didn't really matter to us.

All the while, I was respectful of the natives' cultural attitudes toward the white man, beyond their appreciation of his medical care. Friendly, yes. Fraternization, no. It was the most platonic connection I have ever experienced.

I spoke the same universal language with Myai as I did with the natives who stood in the primitive,

The Country Doctor

dispensary, sick-call line and those who filled the hospital beds.

Speech was difficult because each tribe had its own dialect and, at times, could not even understand each other. The country's official language of Amharic was as foreign to some of them as English, but I became adept enough to understand and try to help. A nod of the head, a certain sound, a look, a touch was as understandable there as anywhere else in the world. I could read what was spoken by their body posture, arm movements, facial expressions, and especially, their eyes.

And I spoke back to them, just by being there. I spoke as with my patients anywhere, from country to town, reservation to city, to African bush country, around the world and back again to mountain country, USA.

Twenty-five years later, country doctoring in Africa is a distant memory, faded, but not forgotten. And, I cherish the memory of a pretty, young girl named Myai.

Feelings are beautiful; try wearing them on the outside.

Interlude 29

Some Finalpourri

Cold temperatures and drafts do not cause colds. Neither do cold, wet feet. It takes a germ to produce infection. If you get so cold as to suffer hypothermia, your general resistance may be lowered and make it more likely for you to succumb to the germ.

Before going to the doctor for cold feet, be sure you don't have holes in your socks.

The cheapest and best throat gargle I've found after forty years of country doctoring is probably in your bathroom medicine cabinet and kitchen. In a half-glass of comfortably hot water, dissolve one-half teaspoonful of salt, one-quarter teaspoonful of baking soda, six drops of tincture of merthiolate, and two crushed aspirin tablets.

Gargle with small amounts of this mixture as far back in your throat as possible. Keep your throat relaxed. Allow the vapors to enter your nasal passages. Use the entire amount and repeat as often as necessary. It is not harmful if you swallow some, but be sure you are not allergic to any of the ingredients.

Chapter 30

Rambling Wrecks

It's amazing that most people are still alive considering the way they live.

"I know I'm not a good patient," Jamie remarked when she stopped me in the parking lot of her work place.

"You don't have to tell me that," I said. "Here you are with abdominal pain that you've had for two years. You could have come to my office any time, you know."

"Well, it wasn't that bad in the beginning," she continued. "It still isn't. I'm just tired of it being there."

"I haven't seen you for this since it started, Jamie, so why don't you tell me more about it."

"It's right here on the right side just below my rib cage. All the while I'm sitting down, it hurts. When I lean forward, it pinches like a needle in there. When I'm standing and stretch back or bend sideways, it wacks me like a fist punch."

"Is it true that you went back to work two days after you had your gallbladder operation, two years ago?"

"Sure it is," she said. "The girls at work needed me. I couldn't let them down. I had to go back, quick."

Alive and Well

Jamie was a group leader in a small shoe factory, and she felt she was indispensable to the successful daily operation of the place.

"And that's not all. My right knee hurts. I can hardly stand after sitting for an hour or two if my leg has been bent in the same position. I limp like a crippled ninety-year old. I feel like I need a cane or a walker.

"All my joints hurt, my back and my hands and my feet. Do you think I might have osteoporosis? Come next month, I'll be fifty years old. And, look at my weight. I'm already too heavy and getting worse right along."

"Well, I'm glad you're not having a cardiac arrest," I said solemnly. "Your family and friends would never survive without you." Then I added with a smile, "And, those thousands of shoes you make every week would be nothing but soleless.

"Jamie," I went on, as firmly as I possibly could in the middle of the parking lot, "you're all fired up about caring for everybody and everything but yourself. You know what you're doing, don't you? You're using up all your time and energy on other things and other people so that you don't have to tend to yourself. You're taking better care of your job than your own body. That's a way of slow suicide. Why don't you call the office for an appointment?"

"Well, maybe I will," she replied, "someday soon."

The Country Doctor

As I walked on toward my office, I heard a familiar racket approaching from two blocks away. At five feet two inches and one hundred ten pounds, twenty-five-year-old Richie had learned to do just about anything with a moving vehicle be it a car, a truck, or a motorcycle. He could tear down an engine and put it back together, and it would work as good as new. Brakes, transmissions, universals, clutches, everything internal to the smooth operation of a moving vehicle was his expertise. He kept the vital organs of his vehicles in the best of condition, but their bodies were a nightmare.

"Richie," I said to him one day, "if you were a physician, I just know you would be an internal medicine specialist, a diagnostician for vital organs."

"Well, thanks," he responded. "I do like tinkerin' and fixin'."

"But, you wouldn't make much of a dermatologist," I teased. The bodies of the vehicles he owned were a terrible sight to see. Rust holes of various sizes and shapes were patched like the torn and tattered jeans he wore. Bumpers were held on with wire thread, windows were cracked or missing, and the entire bodies were a frightful junkyard sight. I often wondered how they held together. Each time I saw him driving by, motor purring like a contented cat, I expected to see the body suddenly fall away from the chassis and scatter all over the road,

Alive and Well

with the sound of a turned-over truck of recycled bed pans. And there sat Richie behind the steering wheel, himself as contented as the car's motor, driving on like nothing had happened.

Richie took care of his physical body in very much the same manner as his moving vehicles. I seldom saw him in my office. He never missed work. He claimed he was never sick. I figured he kept himself going with his own automatic drive of the kind he gave his cars and trucks.

"Richie, I'm reminding you again that you can get away with ignoring your health only when you're a young and footloose blade. It changes as you go along, you know."

"Not for me," he said nonchalantly as his car purred to a start and its body rattled noisily away.

Forty years later, I am still amazed at how often and how well the body heals itself without medical intervention. Millions of people somehow survive in spite of themselves.

Wear out or you'll rust out.

Interlude 30

Bumps and Bruises

A bruise is a black and blue spot in the skin. A bump, or contusion, is some kind of external pressure against the body that causes capillaries and small veins to break open.

The simple pressure of leaning against a chair, a doorway, an appliance, or the like may cause black and blueness several days later.

Vessels can rupture spontaneously. This is more common in women since the female hormones can increase the fragility of the capillary walls. On the elderly, skin thins and drys, capillaries weaken and become prone to bleeding.

Bruise marks can also be a side effect of certain medications such as cortisone, Coumadin®, and some of the medicines purchased over the counter.

Bruises should not be confused with bleeding underneath the skin or inside the body. It is a serious matter when blood vessel rupture takes place in an eye, brain, lung, heart, or leg; and it requires prompt medical attention.

Chapter 31

Miss Lottie

I don't want to be dead before I'm gone.

It was always a good idea for me to call ahead so I would not have to wait so long for Lottie to respond to my vigorous rapping at her locked door. Her hearing was very poor and if she were in the back of her big, rambling house, there was no way I would be heard. At the same time, I was never sure she remembered I was coming.

"Well, you can come in, but I'm not sick," Lottie would announce. In a way she was right. She wasn't sick in an urgent or acute sense of the word. At the same time, her eighty-eight years of age brought with them high blood pressure, arthritis, and heart trouble. It was a big chore for her, even with the unwelcome help of her two nieces, to get to the office. She wouldn't make the trip willingly, for she never considered herself anything but well.

"I don't need a doctor, and I don't need your pills," she would say in her soft but determined voice.

I never questioned her opinion. I did question the wisdom of her living alone. So did her few remaining

The Country Doctor

nieces, friends, and neighbors. Her three-story house was spacious enough for a large family with many children.

Lottie was on my list of some several dozen, housebound, elderly or debilitated patients. Their total lives were spent in confinement to their homes. Major effort was required on the part of the patient and family to obtain ordinary care at the hospital or doctor's office. They arrived by way of walker, wheelchair, or ambulance, and the cost of ambulance transportation was no small amount.

It was so much easier to take care of them by regular, house calls once a week. That became a nice diversion from the rigors of a busy office schedule. By the end of the day, I would have seen a dozen or so patients and would have traveled some sixty to eighty miles of the beautiful hills and valleys of the Allegheny Mountains.

Driving along the back roads is a roller-coaster experience. There are as many roads as there are slopes, and each connects the ridge top with its bottom land. Those unfamiliar with the area could easily get lost. However, there is an old bit of sage advice which says, "When lost in the labyrinth of mountain country roads, you will eventually come out somewhere if you just keep following the valley." It is the same as following a stream on foot, ever downward into increasingly larger streams and lakes and rivers. In those mountains, it could be as

Alive and Well

far away as the Chesapeake Bay, but at least you would know where you were.

Miss Lottie had outlived all ancestors, three spouses, all siblings, even some of her children and grandchildren. Often, the elderly on my rounds had no one left save distantly-related nieces and nephews, most of whom lived great distances away. So many of my patients truly are all alone. Their only human connection may be a few close friends or caring neighbors.

My house-call circuit took me to Lottie's place once a month to check her blood pressure, listen to her heart, and comfort myself that she was all right. It was the only way I could be sure she was taking her medication as prescribed. Whether or not she was, I could not depend on her family to tell me, Lottie simply would not confide in them. She was always quick, concise, and clear to say, "I don't need you to tell me what to take, and I can take care of my house and myself."

In the early days of our acquaintance, I had relied on my office receptionist to make arrangements for my visits. They had to be far enough in advance to prepare her mind for accepting me. They could not be too far ahead, however, or she would not remember. In any event, she was always astonished to see me.

The Country Doctor

"Oh, it's you!" she would say with a surprised tone in her little voice as I chuckled my way into her home and fondly gave her a hug.

I would then wait at least five minutes while, without a word, she made her slow and deliberate trip to the bathroom, inserting her dentures before she would talk to me. Her blood pressure and pulse were always better with her teeth in place. She heard better with her eye glasses on, too.

Lottie was indeed independent enough to demand that she live in her own home and by her own self. No one ever doubted her wishes. Myself, I questioned the sense of it and wondered how often her nieces were really checking up on her. She was as cantankerous about the necessity of my visit as she was about her nieces' opinion of her lifestyle.

"I'll dress as I want and I'll clean my house when I think it's necessary," was her regular refrain.

Lottie's house was located just a half mile away. I could see her place from the back window of my office. Ashbury Street runs along the edge of the lake and the town park. The lake is in the center of the village and its two thousand residents. Susquehoning is surrounded on all sides by deciduous, tree-covered hills that reach upwards some four hundred to seven hundred feet. Many small streams flow out of the valleys and converge into two large ones that form Mirror Lake.

It was a very picturesque centerpiece for the town dwellers, visitors, and for Lottie. However, the closest she ever got to the outdoors was her front porch.

Lottie's favorite spots in her rambling home were the bed, the bathroom, the kitchen table, the reclining chair at the front window, and the porch swing. When the weather was suitable for her frail, eighty-eight body years, I would see her there, rocking and looking out over the lake.

She navigated the first floor by using a narrow pathway between the five rooms. There was a pretty stained-glass window that lightened up a somewhat gloomy dining room. It appeared a bit out of place in the old home until I used my imagination to envision it fifty years earlier. The furnishings had come down through several generations of the family.

Lottie herself no longer saw much uniqueness or value to her antique possessions nor did she care. But I was sure that one or more of her distant relatives had a sharp eye on them.

The one piece I had became most fond of, although it was not an antique, was an old, nondescript floor lamp that stood by a wall desk in the living room. As I would take Lottie's blood pressure and listen to her heart, she

The Country Doctor

would stand by the lamp, remove its shade, turn the switch, and go through her methodic ritual of replacing a burnt-out light bulb.

"Now we can see better," she would announce. I never questioned whether or not we could.

The only time Miss Lottie sat for me--she was too busy to sit otherwise--was when it was necessary for me to clip her toenails. She was halfway willing to submit to a clipping every three months or so after the nails had penetrated through her slippers. Without footwear, the nails would curve downward to the bottom of her toes and cut into the skin. Her nails were always fairly thick and required considerable effort to trim.

One day, Lottie's niece called and asked me to see her aunt because of chest pain and a shaking spell. The call ended as usual with the comment, "She insists she doesn't need you. She may not let you in the house."

I half expected to see the barrel of a shotgun aimed at me from a nearby window on my first few visits, but I soon became courageous enough to rap on the door. Later on, if the door were unlocked, I would let myself in. It was a time-saver for me, since Lottie seldom heard my knocks. I would wander from one room to another looking for her and calling her name, and sooner or later, our paths would cross.

Alive and Well

Eventually, I figured out that she was playing her own little game of independence with everyone, including me. I would catch an occasional, impish, little smile along with a cute twinkle in her eye when she thought no one was looking.

The time finally came when I dared talk to her about living alone. I didn't have much hope that I would be able to convince this strong-minded, little lady that she should not be living by herself, that it would be nice for her to be around other people. A personal-care home within two blocks of her own place had a resident who had been an acquaintance of hers some fifty years earlier.

I had known Lottie for six years, and as the months and years rolled by, everyone concerned with her welfare had come to agree. It had simply become too unsafe and too unhealthy for her to continue living alone. After repeated attempts in the past, we did not expect to meet with success.

I suggested that Lottie visit the nearby personal-care home for a first hand look at the place and its people, meet with her friend of long ago, and then decide for herself. At first, of course, she objected. Then, much to our surprise, she half-heartedly promised to check out the place.

Diane, the young, attractive, neatly-groomed owner of the home accompanied her. On their way back, the two

The Country Doctor

stopped by my office for me to give Lottie the blood pressure and heart check which was required by the home. Miss Lottie was clean and nicely dressed. Her hair had been freshly done, and I told her how pretty she looked.

As we bantered comments about in a jocular vein, and it became a fun visit, I could not resist asking Miss Lottie whom she thought was the cutest of the three of us in the room.

She was quick enough to reply, "Well, considering my age of eighty-eight and you two young kids, I think I am!"

Not one of us doubted that Lottie, indeed, was the cutest of all.

That visit did the trick. Lottie actually agreed to try the place out. Even though she walked out on several occasions, finding her way back to her own home two blocks away, she settled in and did well. I can't say she was always sweet, but she was definitely cute with her strong-minded, independent, and cantankerous ways. And, we all loved her.

While making my weekly nursing-home calls, I have often reflected on the nursing-home scene. The setting sometimes works for the good of the patient, but sometimes, for the bad. In earlier days, the places left much to be desired. Heat, lighting, safety, comfort, cleanliness, food, and nursing conditions were often inadequate and inferior.

A few years back, my own mother, eighty-seven then, resided in a personal-care home. Each visit with her was a special one, not just because she was my mother, but because she was an individual with a unique personality. Within a very short time after her arrival at the place, her sunny personality, her smiles, and her friendliness had earned her the reputation of sweetheart of the home.

Our visits were always filled with good thoughts and feelings, touch, humor, and heart-filled nostalgia. I knew those visits were important to her. They gave her something to which she could look forward and boosted her physical and mental well-being. That was not the case with many other people living there or in dozens of similar places.

In the absence of familiar faces and voices and touch, mental and physical deterioration can happen quickly in such institutions. The elderly need the stimulation of conversation to recollect the past, connect with the present, and hope for the future. Without it, nursing home residents move less and sit more. As they do, they simply sit and stare until their heads fall in resignation. Eventually they stare at the floor, then close

The Country Doctor

their eyes as they further withdraw into themselves to avoid the pain and sadness of emptiness and meaninglessness.

Fortunately, time has changed this setting in today's medical and social scene. Social activities, crafts, birthday and holiday celebrations are all part of the changing picture.

Nursing home residents' faces smile and eyes brighten from the physical and mental stimulation of volunteer visits, whether they are by singing and dancing groups or by their own friends and family. Nothing lights up their faces as much as the view of a small child or a baby who goes by their door or who visits at the next bed.

It is wonderful that some nursing homes now allow dogs and other animals to make daily pet rounds to the residents' rooms. They and I both know they are doing those dear folks more good than the nurse or the doctor ever could.

Miss Lottie lived to a pretty nice ninety years. Throughout her stay, she remained mobile and able to care for her own personal self. I wish as much for myself someday.

How old would you be if you didn't know how old you were?

Interlude 31

Wrinkles

To be alive is to live, to live is to get older, and to get older is to get wrinkles. There is no way to get from birth to death without them unless death is premature, and that's the last thing most of us want.

How soon wrinkles appear for each of us, and how noticeable they become, depends on heredity and the natural aging process.

The natural aging process can be greatly accelerated, however, by the way we eat, sleep, speak, and exercise.

Unnatural aging of the skin comes about by excessive exposure to the sun. Certain disease conditions can also accelerate wrinkling. So, too, can the way we use our faces to express our thoughts, feelings, and behavior. Tobacco smokers accelerate the aging of their skin to the extent that a heavy smoker at age forty has the wrinkle equivalence of age sixty.

You can help yourself by avoiding excessive sun and not smoking. Keep your facial muscles soft and relaxed as much as possible. Smile more, squint less, have a sweet attitude instead of a sour face. Use natural moisturizing creams and lotions. Light massage and gentle touch go a long way, too.

While psychological advice can be helpful for balding and graying, the easiest, cheapest, and most effective thing you can do for wrinkling is to accept it. Besides, if you let your pleasing personality shine through, most people won't even notice them.

Chapter 32

A Pint's a Pound

Too many square meals can make you round.

"Well, Jamie," I remarked. "I hear you say you wish you could lose weight. We both know you should."

At three hundred twenty pounds and a height of five feet two inches, Jamie sat in my examining room telling me for the nth time she wanted to lose weight.

"Yes," she said, "and I could, too."

"But I still don't hear you say you're going to."

"Well, I wish I would," she said once again, in a pensive sort of way.

"But I still don't hear you say you will."

"Well, no--oo-o."

"So you won't either, will you?"

Jamie and I were having our usual discussion about her weight, and we were still getting nowhere. I kept hoping that sooner or later it could happen, so I never gave up trying.

It's no secret that obesity is widespread, not just around the waistline, but in every city, town, and village across the United States. Even the rural areas are not immune from the biggest of all maladies that plague humankind.

No socio-economic level is excluded for the overweight patients who enter and leave my office. They are of both genders and range in age from late childhood into the advanced years of adulthood. The affluent, the working poor, the retired, and the wards of the state and federal government are equally affected.

It is the case that, in small towns and rural areas across the nation, where other social and cultural functions are at a minimum, dining out is one of the most popular forms of entertainment.

Overeating is comforting for a great many anxious people, no matter their locale. Obesity is usually due to overeating and under-exercising, in other words, taking in more calories than the body needs for its basal metabolism and its daily mental and physical efforts. Most often, obesity is not due to an underactive metabolism, but an overactive fork. It can be that simple.

For government-supported groups, the working poor, and the underprivileged, excess weight often comes about because of high-calorie, high-fat foods that are big on their menu. Those foods are often tastier and generally cheaper as well.

Alive and Well

During my house call to the Fuller's place, I was once again reminded of how widespread obesity is right in my own backyard.

Louise's family had asked me to visit her because she had been sick with a virus. She couldn't get to the office, because she could not get out of her house. She could not even get out of her room!

When I stepped inside the door, I saw obesity sprawled out all over the entire king-size bed. Louise's body was about to flow off both sides and onto the floor. That is what can happen to a seven hundred and fifty pound body.

I could readily understand why poor Louise could not make it to the office. She was able to make it to the commode only with the help of a hoist.

Her head and shoulders were propped up on a small mountain of pillows. In front of her was a kind of a table top consisting of a one-inch-thick sheet of four-by-eight-foot plywood. It hid the bottom half of both the bed and my patient. Spread out across the surface was a variety of items including a TV set, reading and writing material, and a host of paraphernalia not readily recognizable except for various packages of crackers, cereal, and other food items. A four-foot grappling hook was within arm's reach. I later watched Louise use it to move her legs from one place to another on the bed.

The Country Doctor

Louise's daughter asked me to check a rash on her mother's legs. It took me some time to find a recognizable extremity. It was not possible to take her blood pressure, but I found her pulse over the upper left side of her chest after a diligent search with my stethoscope. There was no hint of a pulse at her wrist or ankle. There was just too much fatty tissue between her arteries and my palpating fingers.

The mystery of her rash was the one thing that was pretty easy to solve. Most of the skin on the inner part of both legs, from the ankles to the groin was excoriated from the constant rubbing together of the skin surfaces. It was a bit less simple for me to try to do anything about it.

Once again, Jamie returned to my office, and once again, her desire to lose weight had been piqued by my previous comments.

"I'm going to assume you're serious, Jamie. We don't need to waste our time or your money on this visit if you aren't."

She assured me that she was, and so, I continued.

"I'll tell you once more that to lose weight you must consider what you eat minus what you burn. That means common sense, calorie control, and physical fitness. Keep

Alive and Well

in mind that 3,500 hundred calories equals one pound of weight. Losing weight is an everyday affair. Keeping it off is a lifetime commitment.

"Look at it this way," as I put a reassuring arm around her shoulder. "If diabetics do not pay close attention to calories, they commit relatively sudden suicide. Heavy people do the same thing at a slower rate. We all know that obese people are much more subject to diseases like high blood pressure, arthritis, strokes, heart attacks, cancer, and kidney failure.

"Jamie," I went on, as I patted her hand. "You don't need books or diet shots or special food supplements. Those things are out there for someone's profit, and you won't find any magic wands.

"Vitamins, minerals, and special foods, all the way from amino acids to zinc and from mega doses to macro-prices, will guarantee you a flat pocketbook and healthy bathroom plumbing."

She was listening and laughing with her eyes.

"And don't forget about liquids. Caloric drinks such as milk, soda, and alcohol are a quick and easy way to overload yourself. An average serving of most of them loads you with two to three hundred calories."

"Wow, I didn't realize that!" Jamie exclaimed. For the first time in all the years I've known her, she seemed more interested and ready to commit.

The Country Doctor

"Okay," she asked. "I've read that drinking lots of water can help a person to lose weight. What do you say to that?"

"It can help to fill your stomach so there is less room for food, but you have to remember that even plain water has weight," I continued.

"All right," questioned Jamie, "how much does a quart of water weigh?"

"Let's look at water and other calorie-free liquids in terms of pounds," I suggested, "We'll check with the pharmacist first."

The pharmacist's opinion is the last word for me when it comes to the chemical names of medicines, their side effects, and questions about weights and measures.

Although I learned a great deal about such matters during my medical training, I don't always remember the details. I knew I could depend on the pharmacist for a quick and accurate answer. I figured it would be an easy question for him.

"Peter," I began, after he responded to my phone call. "I'm in need of your help with a quick question."

"Okay, what is it?" he asked.

"I need to know the weight of a pint of water. I'm working on a weight-loss plan for a patient who's in my office."

Alive and Well

"How much does a pint of water weigh?" he repeated. "Just plain water?"

"Yes, plain water or any other calorie-free beverage such as tea, black coffee, diet soda. What would be the weight?"

"Okay, let me think. A pint is sixteen ounces. And, there are about thirty grams in an ounce, so there are one thousand grams in a quart. And a quart is two pints." On and on he went.

"I think the answer is, uh, so many ounces," Peter finally muttered. "But just a minute. I'll check my book of weights and measures."

"I need your answer in pounds, Pete."

Five minutes later he was back on the phone.

"Here we are Doc. I'm looking it up right now. Hmm, da-da-d-da-a-ump. Gallons. Quarts. Pints. Ounces. Grams. Now let me see. Aha!" he shouted. "I've got it. I just remembered what my grandmother told me years ago. It's a pound! She used to say, "A pint's a pound the world around!"

When weight increases inch by inch, the clothes respond pinch by pinch.

Interlude 32

Common Sense and Your Weight
Some Helpful Highlights

1. WAT-U-R equals WAT-U-EAT minus WAT-U-BURN.
2. 3,500 calories = one pound of weight.
3. One quart of fluid = two pounds.
4. Components of a commonsense diet = a balance of carbohydrates + proteins + fat + calorie-free liquids.
5. Excessive intake of mega vitamins (A-Z) + minerals (AA-Zinc) = a flat wallet and healthy bathroom plumbing.
6. Weight loss and normal weight maintenance = 50% calorie control + 50% fitness.
7. Fitness = daily balanced attention to physical, mental, and spiritual well-being.
8. Estimating desirable body weight (DBW), regardless of age.

Alive and Well

Build	Women	Men
Medium	100 pounds. for first 5' of height plus add five pounds per inch above 5'	106 pounds for first 5' of height plus add six pounds per inch above 5'
Small	Subtract 10%	Subtract 10%
Large	Add 10%	Add 10%

9. Rate of weight loss = number goal + time goal.
10. Common sense rate for weight loss = 1 to 3 lbs. per week.
11. Weight loss of 1 lb. per week = 500 calories less per day.
12. Example: Present Weight   200 pounds
             Weight Goal   180 pounds
             Pounds to Lose   20 pounds
             Time Goal (weeks) At one pound a week = 20 weeks, about five months

This can be accomplished by decreasing calorie intake by 3,500 calories a week = 500 calories a day = one desert.

Chapter 33

Tell Me a Story

*If you don't have a heart full of love,
you have the worst kind of heart trouble.*

Mirror Lake glistened before us like a jewel in the palm of the surrounding mountains. In lush spring foliage, the scene and the mood were made for the moment, and so were we.

"Tell me another story," Barbie asked as we sat together in the quiet afternoon of a picture-perfect day in June.

The water's edge snuggled against the surrounding ridges with the intimacy of a kitten tongue lapping its downy-soft calico coat. When all else was quiet, the lake's interface could be heard purring against the tenderloins of the slopes. It was such an essential part of the hills and valleys.

At the edge of the lake, where the stream slowly flowed in from the valley, the natural world fused into the heart-essence of life. A white-tailed deer stood there with front feet and muzzle submerged beneath the water's surface. It epitomized the lake's nurturing of the land's

Alive and Well

green-growing plants and blossoming wildflowers with a fellowship that commonly denominated them.

My Sweetheart and I were a very picnicking pair in those youthful days of our togetherness. Between our own work schedules and living spaces, and in the absence of a home of our own, we picnicked at least once or twice a week. After ten years, we just knew that we had broken the world record for picnics than any other couple in the history of the world. You can be sure those picnics were nestled within the lakes and streams and the hills and valleys of mountain country.

"What would you like to hear about?" I asked.

"Anything," Barbie replied. "You have so much to talk about. The experiences of your childhood, your life as a country doctor, the Native Americans, Africa."

"Well, I don't always want to talk about medical things nor problems nor tragedies. You hear enough of that from me in bits and pieces every day. I'd rather forget about business at a sweet time like this with a girl like you."

"You talk and I'll listen," she remarked in her special childlike way.

"Then I'll tell you one of my lifetime, favorite fairy tales.

"It was the middle of May, and I had just written a prescription for myself to go to the mountains. I was to

The Country Doctor

take full dosage, with all my senses, all day long. It was my favorite medicine with which to treat my body, my mind, and my soul, the best tranquilizer I knew.

"I'm very much like you, Barbie," I remarked. "We both like losing ourselves in the woodlands, to become missing to the rest of the world without really being lost.

"Remember my telling you how I was reputed the best equipped, most experienced, and the least successful hunter in the county in my hunting days past? It was not for the lack of good vision and hearing. I just became mesmerized by the sights, the sounds, the smells, the touch, and the feel of this glorious natural world.

"And so, I followed my prescription.

"And, it happened again.

"I quickly became intoxicated by the sights and the sounds and the fragrances, the murmuring breezes, the music of the birds, the fragrance of green and growing things. I was immersed in a symphony for all my senses. I was living inside an enchanting Monet woodscape.

"In no time at all, the Rip van Winkle syndrome overcame me and I fell into a deeply peaceful sleep. And in that sleep, I dreamt of elves and fairies, of soft sweet music and dance. I was a blissful part of it all. Near the end of the most pleasantly possible of springtime afternoons, I awoke, and I was thoroughly lost. I could not remember how I came to that place, nor did I know the way out. And, at that moment, I really didn't care all that much.

"I was caught up in an incomparable scene of transition from the tattered edges of winter into the full-blown spring of Appalachian Mountain country. The sky was sporting more blue since the clouds had changed from dull gray to white puffs and wisps and streaks. Tree-covered hills had been transformed into a vivid, virile green. Wildlife had shaken off the shackles of hibernation. Wintering chickadees and jays were rousting about and songbirds had returned. Tanagers, orioles, buntings, and warblers filled the air spaces like one, grand, mobile flower garden.

"Dewdrops hung from leaf and blade and reflected woodland shade and shadow, each one mirroring the magic and mystery of mountain country's rhythm and reason. I held the scene close to my heart for a fleeting moment, then set it free for another time and place.

"Through the air like the whispers of a soft breeze, a special fragrance came to me. It filled all space not already occupied by flora and fauna. It perfused all that was not form and color or sound and movement. It captured my heart and filled my soul with ecstasy, as it radiated from the pink-petaled, mountain azalea. It captured my memory for all time.

The Country Doctor

"All creatures seemed to respond to that vision, that aroma, the softness of The Mountain Princess. A rainbow of colors streamed from the tips of her fingers and toes as red bleeding hearts, orange paint brush, yellow trefoil, emerald green grass, pastel bluets, wild geraniums, and violets, to dance through the woodlands in celebration of her pronouncement of another spring. Her petals glowed with the pastel pigments of the world's most beautiful of sunrises and sunsets.

"Now, this is strange, I thought. The sweet-smelling azalea honeysuckle is not due to blossom for another two weeks. Yet, I cannot mistake its haunting, intoxicating, spicy aroma.

"Its powerful attraction lured me in its direction. As the fragrance became increasingly stronger, I could not resist, nor did I want to. I realized it was an extension of my dream. I continued through the bushy undergrowth of the forest, and suddenly found myself in a small clearing.

"And there you were, standing inside a mountain azalea bush, hallowed by a grand bouquet of delicate pink blossoms!

"You moved. You smiled. And, you were real. I was no longer lost. You had found me, and I had found you. We had found each other.

Alive and Well

"We have loved each other twelve months more every year since, and I know you are the Princess of the Mountains for all seasons.

"Next time, I will tell you another of my favorite stories about the Snow Princess. So, did you enjoy my story?" I asked. "Barbie? Barbie?"

There was no answer when I turned in her direction. Barbie was fast asleep, and I knew from the sweet expression on her pretty azalea-pink cheeks that she was living in that same dream from which I had just come.

A fairy tale is a wish on its way to becoming a want.

Interlude 33

I Can Believe That

It's nothing new on the self-help scene that a mixture of honey, lemon, and whisky makes a good hot toddy for coughs, colds, and fever. The potion has been popular for a long time, and with those three ingredients, I can believe it always will be.

I have heard it said that rubbing the inside of a banana peel on the rash of poison ivy relieves itching. I haven't tried it myself, but I do know that if you eat all those bananas, they will be good for your potassium requirement. Also, you should be able to climb trees quicker and scratch your armpits easier.

Citrus fruit farmers guarantee that a few drops of lemon squeezed into the mouth first thing in the morning and every few hours during the day will rid a person of nausea, whatever the cause. It certainly puckers the salivary glands and stomach so that the nausea is forgotten.

Chapter 34

David and Goliath

*Make the most of all that comes
and the least of all that goes.*

"What the Devil's going on with you, David?" I almost shouted. "You are so anemic it's a wonder you can stand. This blood test confirms that your hemoglobin is drastically low! It's only twenty percent of what it should be. Any lower and you would have been crawling in here or wheeled in on a stretcher. How long have you been feeling this way?"

"About six months now," he replied, "It wasn't bad at first, but I've gotten so weak and so tired over the past few weeks that I can barely walk. My endurance level is zero, and I'm sleeping all the time."

"You're pale as a ghost. What have you been doing to get into such a fix? Are you bleeding anywhere?"

"Well, I don't know that I am," he answered with a weak, almost inaudible reply.

I hadn't seen any of the Harrington family since our run around with their private little strep throat epidemic that past winter.

The Country Doctor

David's wife, Terry, was with us in the examining room. She looked at him and said in a firm, maternal voice, "Now, tell him about your shoulder. And your stomach. And your leg. Tell him how you've been taking twenty and more ibuprofen tablets a day for pain. I think that's important."

"Twenty a day!" I exploded. "I'll say that's important! Let's have it, Dave. Tell me more about it."

"Well, you know I have this shoulder pain. I've had it ever since I fell off the ladder while working on my Dad's house last year. I caught my arm in a rung as I came down. The doctor told me I tore my rotator cuff."

"Okay, what's been done about it?" I asked. "How has the doctor been treating you?"

"He's not. I was told I would have to have an operation to fix it. You know how scared I am of needles and knives. I just couldn't face it. But it's been hurting a lot. I've been having more and more trouble trying to operate my machine at work. I might have to take a sick leave."

"I do know how you hate needles and medical attention. This is the first time in four years that I've seen you for yourself. I'll bet if you weren't having pain in your leg, you wouldn't be here even now. So, let's find out what this whole thing is all about.

Alive and Well

"Tell me again, you've been taking twenty ibuprofen tablets a day for the past year? For the shoulder pain?"

"Maybe thirty," David sheepishly replied.

I examined his leg as he winced in pain. His discomfort was localized near his left ankle. I saw redness and swelling around the blood vessels. His problem began to make sense. The irritating effects of all the ibuprofen he had been taking for so long had caused bleeding from the lining of his stomach. Blood was seeping into the stomach and on into the intestinal tract so slowly that it could not be seen in his movements.

I did a rectal examination and found the stool to be strongly positive for occult blood, blood that is not visible. Over a period of months, it had caused David to lose about four pints. His blood had become so thin, it simply could not circulate properly and was seeping into the tissues of his leg.

"David," I said, in no uncertain terms, "you've got to forget about work for now. You could collapse at any minute. You could have a stroke right now. You're going to the hospital! Terry will take you there from here. You are not to drive. I don't want you to do anything but walk from the office to your car. I'll call ahead and have you admitted as soon as you get there."

The Country Doctor

"I've need to go home first," David insisted. "I want to go to the job first thing in the morning to tell them what's going on. Then I'll go."

No amount of pleading could change his mind. His fear of needles and hospitals and doctors was so overwhelming that it came close to killing him.

Very early the next morning, Terry called. She was exceedingly distraught.

"Dr. John, David collapsed when he got up this morning! He's in a faint and I can't get him up!"

"Call the ambulance right away," I demanded. "This can't wait another minute. Get him to the hospital Emergency Room as quick as possible. I'll call ahead. They'll be waiting for him."

By the time he reached the hospital, David had suffered a heart attack for the same reason his leg had pained him the day before. His heart muscle was not getting enough oxygen, so it simply gave up the struggle. He no sooner got to the Cardiac Critical Care Unit than he stroked out. A blood vessel on the left side of his brain let loose, paralyzing him on his right side. At that point, the problem was so complicated and so critical that he had to be flown by helicopter to the tertiary care medical center seventy miles away.

After two weeks and six transfusions of whole blood later, David recovered enough to go home. Over the ensuing months, he slowly improved with a lot of left-over disability.

Winter came and Terry decided to take David to California for further convalescence, for David as well as herself. During their second week there, I received another urgent call at home.

"Doctor," Terry pleaded, again with urgency and distress in her voice. "David's in trouble again."

"What is it?" I asked, equally concerned that he could be experiencing a second heart attack or stroke.

"It's his stomach this time," Terry replied. "He woke up in the middle of the night in extreme pain all over the abdomen. He is bloated and he can't breathe or lie still."

With crossed fingers, I asked, "Is he all right in his chest and his head? Is there any sign of heart or stroke trouble?"

"No, no!" she insisted. "It's all below his chest and in his abdomen. He's been distressed in his stomach during the past few days with some nausea and loss of appetite. What shall we do? Shall we come right home so you can take care of him?"

"Terry," I advised, "this sounds too acute and too severe to chance. Take him to the nearest emergency room and have the doctor call me. I'll fill him in on David's medical history, and we'll decide what to do."

The Country Doctor

It didn't take long to find out that David had unknowingly developed a large, hiatal hernia of his stomach through his diaphragm, a problem unrelated to his previous condition. The stomach had become twisted and squeezed by the diaphragm and was on its way to becoming strangulated. After diagnosis and treatment, David was able to finish out the family's vacation before returning home.

January 2, 1991

Dear Dr. John,

Once again we want to let you know how much we appreciate your compassionate, comforting way. Thank you for your guidance and for talking with the doctors in California on our behalf. Thank you for willingly sharing your holiday season to help us out. We needed reassurance during that difficult time and you provided it and gave the California doctors all the information needed so that David got the best care possible.

Alive and Well

We also thank your lovely wife, Barbie, who shares your life and encourages you. She is beautiful inside and outside and willingly shared her holiday time to help us.

You and Barbie were one of our main blessings this holiday season. Words fail to convey the depth of gratitude we feel toward you both!

Thank you so much,

David and Terry

After returning home, a consultation with the surgeon at the regional medical center led to prompt repair of David's diaphragm. It took a very large incision through the upper abdomen and the rib cage to accomplish the job.

Once again, David gradually recovered. Over the next two years, his life was uneventful for any major problems. He continued to have constant pain, however, from his shoulder, his chest incision, the stroke's damage to his right arm and leg, and the residual effects of the inflammation on his left leg.

As a result, David became increasingly dependent on prescription pain relievers. His dependency on pain medication was a serious concern, and it became necessary to refer him to a chronic pain management clinic. Along with many other treatments, he had to endure a series of injections for control of the various sources of his pain.

Concern subsided once again as David, Terry, and I settled down to deal with an extremely high lipid in his blood, something important in preventing further heart and stroke problems.

It took me quite a while to calm my own fearful expectations each time I heard from Terry or saw David's name on my office schedule. I had a constant worry about what else could possibly happen. Just as my concerns were gradually waning, a recurrent, inguinal hernia required major repair with reinforced wire mesh. That was followed within a month with a gall stone problem that was corrected by laparoscopic surgery.

I continue to see David about every three months, and each time we sit across the desk from each other, I am amazed that this man, who has experienced such incredible misfortune, is still alive. I am equally impressed with his capacity to accept his plight.

This is not to say, by any means, that he is not profoundly frustrated with his multiple disabilities and his chronic pain. David's acceptance, without resignation, is as admirable as his remarkable physical capacity to have lived through it all.

"David," I remarked, not for the first time nor the last, "you are a miracle of survival. In all my forty years of practice, I know of no one else whose body could handle all the physical insults you've had over the past six years. Nor, do I know of anyone whose sanity could have stood up to your ordeal. You are, indeed, a physical, mental, and spiritual survivor. Only your wife, Terry, is the equal of you. You know, I dearly love you both, even though you still cringe and wince at the mention of a needle!"

Slow suicide is like hanging;
it can ruin your health.

Interlude 34

Cabin Fever

Cabin fever is a midwinter dis-ease that strikes its victims a few weeks after January's winter thaw. Most of us are affected to varying degrees with symptoms of restlessness, irritability, tenseness, anxiety, impaired memory, poor concentration, depression or insomnia.

Pre-existing conditions, such as high blood pressure, diabetes, arthritis, and gastritis, may also be aggravated.

Cabin fever is caused by a suppression of the physical, mental, and spiritual energies which we normally vent with our mental and physical activities during the rest of the year. Too much inactivity, overeating, and excessive passive entertainment from television, home videos, and computers play a big part.

The condition gradually dissipates in late March to early April as sap rises in trees and in our own circulatory system.

It can be prevented by keeping your body, mind, and soul coming and going for all seasons.

Chapter 35

Flatlanders and Ridgerunners

*Love fails not when you don't get it,
but when you don't give it.*

After an eight year acquaintance with Roxy and Chuck, I still was not sure whether they loved to hate or hated to love one another.

Listening to their constant squabbling did, indeed, sound as if, for one reason or another, there was a lot of hate between them. It was always the same, whether they were in the office, on the streets, or at the grocery store. Harsh words, heavily laced with a variety of vulgarities, were their standard form of communication.

Is this a show they're putting on for the rest of us, I wondered, or a game they play?

After I had known them for a while, I decided that they didn't think about their relationship one way or another. Everywhere they went, they put on their show.

This unusual couple migrated to Pennsylvania's north-central mountain country shortly after my own arrival. They were "flatlanders" from "downstate" who had relocated to a more relaxed and scenic place in the

The Country Doctor

mountains. There, they joined the native "ridgerunners" to escape the hassle and hustle of metropolitan living. Beauty and serenity went hand in hand and all around, but it was anything but peaceful around Roxy and Chuck.

They lived and squabbled in a camp-like cottage on the top of Blueberry Ridge, one of the prettiest ridges in Laurel County. Each time I drove by in sight of their place it seemed like the walls were alternately expanding and contracting from the force of the battle inside. Even the roof appeared unsettled. I imagined tongues of flame and wisps of smoke arising from the shingles.

The scene, part imaginary in my own mind and part real, seemed out of place in that beautiful country setting. They had a panoramic view from the hilltop, reaching to the horizon over verdant hills and valleys, the surrounding land a patchwork quilt of woodlands, fields, and meadows.

The community of Susquehoning is nestled in the bottomland six miles to the northeast, where a half dozen valleys emerge from between a series of ridges. It was born a lumbering town in the latter half of the nineteenth century, located by a stream that was converted to a small river every spring by a series of jack dams. Logs would then be transported to the Susquehanna River, sixty miles away.

Alive and Well

Back in the pristine forests of the 1800's, towns of two to three thousand people fostered smaller settlements within a radius of ten to fifteen miles. Each was strategically located at the confluence of two or more smaller ridges that allowed ready access to the rich crop of hardwood trees on the slopes.

After the turn of the century, the mountains were raped to the bare earth and the lumbering towns gradually disappeared from the scene. In their heyday, each village had its own church, school, and general store. Decrepit frame houses, a lot of naked foundations, scattered small tanneries, chemical plants, and railroads that had been sired by the lumber mills in the days of robust and frenzied timbering, are the only remaining vestiges of those times.

Roxy and Chuck were in a front row center seat of this mountain-top brigadoon for all seasons. They didn't notice it, though. They were too busy scrapping with each other, looking at each other's foibles, and never seeing the wonderful world all around.

Flatlander immigrants sometimes brought with them personalities and lifestyles that seemed strange to the local people. Both Roxy and Chuck brought with them physical problems that had supposedly disabled them from gainful employment. They had filed suit for pain and

The Country Doctor

suffering and had received sufficient monetary settlement to enable them to retire to the mountains.

After an accident had permanently damaged his legs, big burly Chuck had to retire from the heavy equipment business he had owned. As I became increasingly acquainted with him, I heard a lot about his tribulations as a Viet Nam combat soldier.

"I really hated that place," he said, on more occasions than one. "And I especially hated the @!*#! Army."

"Is that why you stayed in for only ten years instead of twenty?" I asked, thinking he would have stayed until he retired if not for his leg injury.

"I hated it all," he repeated. "I hate people too. I hate everything."

It was just a little curious to me that I always saw Chuck, in the office or anywhere else in town, dressed to the hilt in combat clothes all the way from boots to cap.

Roxy was her own kind of person, with a weighty two hundred forty pounds of robust body and personality. As much as she complained of Chuck's verbal and physical abuse, she never seemed to be in any serious danger. She was big enough and staunch enough to handle Chuck without any trouble, and not just because of his bad legs. I suspect she was tough enough that she could have made a pretty respectable, combat soldier herself.

Alive and Well

Barbie and I, in pleasant conversation, had just driven past Roxy and Chuck's place without realizing it. Chuck spotted us as I saw him out of the corner of my eye. He was outside running his huge tractor on a small lawn. I had wanted to talk to Chuck about looking for something for us in the "big city" on one of their frequent return trips. I decided it would be as good a time as any for Barbie to meet this mismatched couple. I could see the Chunker grin again as we turned around at the next pull-off.

Chuck, dressed as usual in his military camouflage garb, was just tickled to have us visit and even more delighted when Barbie opened up her arms in an affectionate hug.

"Will you come in and sip some cool lemonade? Or, can I mix you something stronger?" Chuck offered as Roxy opened the door. Our hugs, barely reaching around Roxy's reverse hour-glass middle, warmed her even more than the already hot day.

Their home had a cluttered (but identifiable) kitchen, a living room, and one bedroom. Chuck was in the process of putting on an additional room. In front of the unfinished wall, half hidden by a menagerie of things, was a piece of furniture of some kind. The bench in front was filled with ammunition and covered with miscellaneous hunting gear.

The Country Doctor

Barbie's penetrating eye and sweet sense of music identified an old pump organ, almost completely hidden by guns and clothes.

"Oh, what a sight!" Barbie exclaimed. "Whose is it? Where did you get it? What are you going to do with it?"

I knew she was excited about the find and was trying hard not to show it.

"Well, it's ours," Chuck answered. "You remember your patient, Benny Jackson, who died of cancer two weeks ago? In days long past, Benny's wife was the musician in the family. She played for him on this grand, old organ. He wanted us to have it. That's where it came from. I don't know what we're going to do with it. So far, it has been a storage rack for my hunting gear. Neither 'what's her name' nor I can play, and we don't like organ music enough to want to learn."

Barbie swallowed hard, still trying to contain her excitement. Her eyes and hands were fondling the organ's fine walnut wood with appreciation and affection, yearning to give the finish a good cleaning and polishing. She was too choked up to talk, so I asked for her.

"It sounds like you want to get rid of it, Chuck. How much do you want for it?" I could tell Barbie was already figuring out where to put it in our over-cramped apartment.

Alive and Well

Chuck thought for a moment. "As soon as I finish the room and put all this junk away, Doc, you can have it just for getting it out of our way."

"We'll take it. Just let us know when you're ready."

Barbie had not been able to say a word but she didn't need to. I could see the joy on her face as she smiled widely and beamed sweetly at the three of us. It took another several minutes after we left for her to settle herself and talk again.

As we walked away, the shouting began inside, seeming to take up just exactly where it had left off when we first entered the door a half hour before.

At that moment, I guessed it would never be any different for that unique pair and their strange relationship. After all their years together, it would end for them loving to hate each other and hating each other to death.

*We have only one person to blame
and that's each other.*

Interlude 35

I Can Believe That, Too

One small glass of warm milk containing a teaspoonful of sugar and black pepper is said to cure the runs.* If you can manage to swallow the mixture, I can believe it just might work.

I definitely believe garlic can work to prevent virus colds. After all, it keeps people far enough apart to prevent spread of the germs.

A country patient gave me his personal recipe for coughs and colds. Mix ground horseradish with equal parts of honey and take one teaspoonful of the mixture every three to four hours. I can believe that, for I've never seen a radish with a runny nose and I've never heard a bee cough.

* Runs: a nickname for the "back door trots," an expression popularized at the turn of the century when victims with diarrhea trotted to the outhouse on the run.

Chapter 36

The Healing Woods

Yesterday is only a memory. Today is a living moment.

  The way of my weekly house calls was a winding one on that mid-April day of incipient spring. It was a deliberate, long shortcut from the northern side of White Oak Ridge to its southern face where Happy Town lay in serene solitude along Elk Creek, a branch of the Susquehanna watershed. At 800 feet from the foot and 2,400 feet above sea level, I felt on top of the world and could see forever over the everlasting hills and valleys. The slopes and summits were entirely covered with leafless trees, except for small patches of evergreens resembling tufts of hair on a balding head. The somber winter-gray of naked limbs and branches had given way to a modest silver sheen. An occasional blossoming shadbush tree stood out in bright white contrast.

  Two distinct color crowns had been sponge-painted across the broad breast of the ridges. One belonged to the maple trees and was a pretty reddish hue, like a virginal blush on the cheeks of a young girl. The other was a radiant greenish-yellow, the chartreuse of promising, young oak buds.

Chickadee Lookout was a favorite place for putting my feet down to ground myself where all plant and animal life, including my own, begins and ends. Beneath the broad canopy of trees, a floral fantasy had come to life on the faded, leaf-brown, forest floor. Trout lilies stabbed their way up through previous year's leaf fall. They seemed to be testing the new year's temperature, moisture, and light intensity with their freckle-faced rich green blades. As soon as they had been satisfied that conditions were just right, a bright yellow flower would pop out at the top of the stems to take command of further growth and call for others to follow.

Hepaticas, trillium, pink and lavender-blue toothworts, dandelions, and multi-blue violets shimmered across the forest floor like sheets of sparkling jewels flipped off the tip of a fairy godmother's magic wand.

Early morning dew collected at leaf edges and twig tips like tiny tears on cheek and lash. They dangled there for a while, caught in a brief moment of living time. A particular dewdrop attracted me. I peered at it as though into and through a porthole of pure crystal. It reflected a vision clear and clean. I felt witness to the innermost depths of life and living for all creation.

Alive and Well

After a half hour of filling my heart with the sense of awakening life, I was back with my Chunker, drifting slowly down the road to the bottomland near the entrance to Hemlock State Park and the Gordon's home. My purpose was to see Cora for a routine visit and share her grief over Henry's death a year earlier. Along the way, I thought back to my first connection with the two of them.

I had no more settled in to my first year of country practice when I had received an urgent call from Cora.

"Doc, can you come to the house right away? My husband is having bad pain in his low back. He's on the floor. Can't get up. Just can't move. He's in severe pain."

"Well, if you can't get him onto the couch or bed, just make him comfortable on the floor. I'll come right away."

The Chunker and I had put on the speed and fifteen minutes later, I had entered the Gordon's very large, very old, sky-blue farm house. Henry was lying immobile on the living room floor. It was very apparent that he had severe back pain, and that it was running down the back of his leg all the way to his foot. A disk had ruptured in the lumbosacral area and was pressing hard on the sciatic nerve.

It was the first time I had seen Henry as a patient, and almost before we had said hello to each other, I was putting a needle two inches long into his backside.

The Country Doctor

"I'm sorry to meet you with a needle instead of a handshake, Henry," I had apologized.

In obvious misery, he smiled up at me with grateful eyes that told me of my comforting presence. An injection of prednisone and Xylocaine® into the trigger point of his pain had put him back on his feet after a few minutes.

Two operations, dozens of studies, many specialist consultations and physical therapy treatments, many pain pills, and thirty years later, we were still meeting like that.

Despite it all, he had maintained an active and full life all along the way. His medium-strength pain pill helped to keep him comfortable enough to make life and work possible.

"Doc, I'm not addicted to these pain pills, am I?" Henry asked occasionally over the years.

"Henry," I would answer, "you've been taking the same pills three times a day for twenty years now. If you were addicted to them, by this time, you would be taking them by the hundreds. You're not even psychologically dependent on them. You just need them for reasonable comfort, that's all."

Henry had more than chronic low back pain. He had a painful shoulder as well, and I became as familiar with that as with his low back. After several years of injection treatments which relieved him for two to three weeks each time, I received a call from Cora one day, the one that I had long wished and waited for.

"Dr. John," she said. "Henry's shoulder is so much better It's been three months since his last injection, and it's the best he's felt for a long time."

I had finally sorted out the problem. There was not one but a combination of three separate conditions, all within the confines of one shoulder and all at the same time: tendinitis in the front, bursitis in the middle, and fibrositis at the back. I had already tried a single injection at two sites. Neither worked. Each of the three sites kept the other aggravated. As one was relieved, another worsened.

I had been sure of my diagnosis on the previous occasion, and I had decided what had to be done. He needed one full dose of prednisone, divided into three equal portions, injected into each of the three sites one right after the other. Immediately afterward, I re-examined each spot and found them no longer tender to my finger pressure. The instant numbness of Xylocaine® mixed with the prednisone had assured me I had hit the right spots. After that had done the trick, I knew Henry felt better for it, and so did I.

Henry's sudden death from a heart attack just a year ago has left a non-refillable void in my heart for the

The Country Doctor

rest of my own life. After thirty-five years, Henry and Cora had become more than patients; they were good friends, and they were family, pure and simple. And, that was the way of it, in the spirit of those country doctoring days a generation ago.

I learned a lot about pain from Henry's experience with it and my experience with him--not the least of which was my own personal anguish at his death. Pain can be physical or mental or spiritual. It can be acute and transient, or it can be chronic and inescapable. Pain can be subjective and felt only by the patient and without proof to others by physical findings or test results. People have different thresholds of tolerance for pain. Like fear, it is the body's way of telling us that something's amiss. It is universal and inevitable. It is one of the most basic of feelings for human life and living.

My own personal wake-up call in my forties allowed for a deeper awareness of basic human feelings that are the foundation of a great inverted pyramid of feelings within each of us. Regardless of the numerous names loosely used by people in general, and patients in particular, I decided there are really only six. At the moment of life's conception, the feeling of JOY appears for the first time in the history of one's existence. It is personified to its ultimate by the young infant and stays

Alive and Well

with us for a lifetime. JOY is the first, after which all five others evolve.

In order to preserve JOY, we become subject to PAIN, a feeling that protects us from harm and preserves our continued well being. When PAIN is sufficiently severe, frequent, and lasting, it gives rise to the feeling of FEAR for our lives and drives us away from PAIN to return again to JOY. FEAR may, also, give rise to the feeling of ANGER which helps us to escape from, or overcome, our FEAR to return again to JOY.

As the feelings of JOY, PAIN, and FEAR develop a relatively stable, mutually satisfactory homeostasis within ourselves and in relationship to our life's circumstances, periodic loss enters the scene. This, then, gives rise to the feeling of GRIEF--the loss of people and things that have been necessary for our physical, psychological, and spiritual well being. Inevitably, the lack of something we find necessary for our mutual well being causes SADNESS to enter our lives.

All six emotions interplay among themselves, back and forth and up and down. This pyramid of human feelings enables us to cope with whatever their cause. When realized and accepted and allowed, they can dissipate and return us always to JOY, the first and most basic and most enduring of feelings.

The Country Doctor

The myriad of other spoken and written words that are called feeling are just substitutes for the basic six:

To be anxious is to know FEAR

To be depressed is to be in mental PAIN

To be frustrated is to be ANGRY

To cry is to know JOY or SADNESS or GRIEF

To dance and laugh and sing is to feel JOY

My extended family of many thousands of people as patients have been equal parts of joy and grief over a half century of time. Neither joy nor grief would have been mine without them.

There's still fun to be had for anyone with low back pain at the nightclub in town called the Slipped Discotheque.

Interlude 36

Trigger Points

Trigger points are "hot spots" of pain which result from inflammation in muscle tissue. There may be one or more fingertip-sized spots of localized tenderness.

Even though pain may radiate into surrounding muscles, it is most often located in the muscles of the neck, shoulders, upper and lower back, hips, thighs, and knees.

Trigger points may be caused by previously bruised or pulled muscle or they may result from the repetitive strain of work efforts. Improper posture can also play a big part, especially in sedentary work.

Persistent trigger points raise the diagnostic question of fibromyalgia, meaning multiple site pain in the fibrous tissues of muscles. It is to be distinguished from arthritis, bursitis, tendinitis, strains, and sprains.

Treatment of trigger points is accomplished by the self help of nonsteroidal, anti-inflammatory medications such as Tylenol® or ibuprofen. Pain killers and steroids are best avoided unless prescribed by a doctor. Moist heat and/or cold applications can help, and deep massage often provides significant relief.

For the best long-term treatment and prevention, muscles require conditioning by stretching and exercise; ongoing physical and mental relaxation also plays a part.

Chapter 37

Live and Let Die

A doctor does well to cure occasionally, relieve often, and comfort always.

"It's been thirty years now since you saved my life, Doc," Ken said as he placed his arm around my shoulders. "And I'm still glad you did."

"Well, I'm happy to hear you say that, Ken," I replied.

Thirty years earlier, I had seen Ken for a routine physical examination and discovered a lump in his thyroid gland. He had no symptoms, no signs of anything amiss. He was unaware of its presence.

"I wonder how long it's been there," he mused when I had told him about it.

"So hard to tell. A few months. Maybe a year or so. These tumors grow so slowly that you wouldn't have detected it on your own for quite a while."

"Anyway, we know it's there, so your thyroid gland needs to be checked by a special x-ray to see if it's an overactive lump or not. If it is, then you will need a biopsy

Alive and Well

to confirm just what kind of lump it is and to decide what to do about it."

A week later, it turned out to be a "hot" cancerous tumor. That meant surgery. After another week, the lump was removed and the cancer was completely eliminated.

When I first met Ken, he had been my daughter's elementary school music teacher. We quickly became good friends. Over the years, we spent time together on occasional weekends and vacations, fishing the small lakes throughout Sandy County. Several trips to northern Ontario were memorable walleye excursions. Pan fried on the banks of the lakes at lunch time, those tasty, fresh-water fish were the ultimate reward. White-tailed deer, upland game bird, and rabbit hunting rounded out a mutually wonderful relationship.

"There's a funny thing about saving lives, Ken," I once said. "Some people want their lives saved and some don't.

Of course, most doctors have saved and prolonged many lives by dedication to their Hippocratic calling through careful listening, thorough examination, and diligent treatment; but it hasn't always been appreciated. It was a surprise for me to learn early on that some people just don't want to go on living. That was something I

The Country Doctor

didn't learn in medical school, but a few years down the road I began to understand.

One day I was walking through an outpatient clinic corridor. The chairs that lined both sides were filled with people waiting to be called into treatment rooms. As I passed an older gentleman, I noticed him suddenly slumping forward on his chair. Sensing that he had just had a cardiac arrest, I rushed to him and thumped his chest a quick and forceful blow.

He quickly sat upright, took a deep breath, stood up, and struck me in the face with his fist. I reeled backwards onto the floor, a bit dazed at the unexpected blow. I shook my head of some lightheadedness and looked up to see a very angry man standing over me saying, "Why did you do that? I was on my way to the light at the end of the tunnel and you brought me back to life!"

What could I say? The man had been well on his way to dying. That's exactly what he wanted, and I had spoiled it for him.

On another occasion, I was taking a blood sample from the arm of a terminally ill cancer patient when he suddenly began to gasp his last breath. He pointed an accusing finger at me saying, "You just killed me!" Before I had a chance to explain otherwise, he passed away.

Alive and Well

I knew without a doubt that the man had not been ready to die, even though his death had been inevitable. I felt sad that I had not had the chance to explain I had merely been taking a blood sample to check his sugar. It has always been my wish to please my patients as much as possible. In his case, I'm sure he was one dissatisfied customer.

People can be strange creatures I reminded myself, and not for the last time. There are those with such severe disease and disability, it's a wonder how they continue to live and why they would want to. Others are in the best of physical health and seem not to care whether they live or die. And then, there are the -holic group of individuals who overeat, overdrink, abuse drugs and tobacco, overuse caffeine, and overwork. They are committers of slow suicide, and unwilling or unable to change.

Thirty years later I, too, was glad Ken was living and well. The surgery had not affected his voice box, and that had been a very special blessing in his case. He was a golden-throated crooner with a small choral group. I had worried about complications until I heard him talk as soon as he was out of anesthesia.

It takes great skill to avoid damage when removing the thyroid gland. There is the risk of injuring the nerve

The Country Doctor

to the voice box adjacent to the thyroid gland. Sometimes it is unavoidable. Should the nerve be cut, the vocal cords become paralyzed and the victim is rendered permanently speechless.

Ken, however, continued to sing his way throughout the countryside for many years after his retirement, much to the delight of a lot of appreciative listeners.

A good laugh and a nap are my favorite cures.

Alive and Well

Interlude 37

Common Sense and Stress Management Some Highlights

1. Stress is normal. Distress is not.

2. Allow yourself the natural feelings of Joy, Pain, Fear, Anger, Sadness, and Grief.

3. Be aware of how you feel and why. Accept your feelings as normal. Allow them to be expressed.

4. Helping yourself.

    a. Physical activity
    b. Share your distress
    c. Take care of your physical self
    d. Make time for fun
    e. Do unto others
    f. Make a list
    g. Don't try to be always right on top
    h. It's okay to cry
    I. Create a quiet scene
    j. Avoid self-medication

5. Relax: Physically, Mentally, Spiritually.

Chapter 38

Happy Town

*I like being eighty years young--
it beats being forty years old.*

Happy Town comes up quickly at the outer side of a right-hand curve on Butternut Road. It can't be missed, and you know you're there as the sign suddenly appears on the left. A one-by-two-foot rectangular sign perches at the top of a four-foot-high post. It is brightly painted with two words, Happy and Town. Underneath each is a yellow smile face and in between the two is U.S.A. I can't help but smile back.

The likes of Happy Town is all that's left of those hardwood lumbering days in north-central Pennsylvania. The old timber towns have degenerated into small clusters of camps and a half dozen trailers huddled close together and perched on the edge of a creek. They erupt on the landscape like cancerous growths on a beautiful scene. Many of them are tumbledown eyesores of dismal design, poorly made, unkempt, and half lost among overgrown grasses and bushes. The dwellings are occupied by hunters and fisherfolk in season and by downstate city

Alive and Well

dwellers at summertime weekends, holidays, and vacation times. They are most often owned by out-of-towners who could care less about the aesthetic beauty of the pristine land.

As I stumbled through the tall, weedy grass to Rosy's cottage, I reflected on the fact that there are a lot of little ol' ladies in my practice that are living out their existence alone in our mountains.

With some good fortune, I had just made it across a tumbledown, wood footbridge that spanned Crooked Creek into what used to be a lawn. Halfway lost in reverie, I was about to take my next step down onto a discarded tire when it suddenly sprung straight out into a long, thick black snake that quickly slithered away into the bordering thicket. I promptly slithered backwards myself for a few moments, catching my second wind to continue on through the overgrown yard.

I mentioned this to Rosy as I guided myself through the maze of scattered furniture, newspapers, magazines, knicks and knacks, and all things unimaginable.

"So you ran into my snake," she remarked with an impish grin. "Just a few days ago I picked it up by its tail, swung it around above my head several times, then let it fly into that field you just came through like a non-returnable boomerang!"

The Country Doctor

I held back a laugh having trouble imagining sweet, little ol' Rosy, at the age of ninety, in poor general health, hard of hearing, with poor eyesight, finding it difficult to stand or walk without the aid of a cane, performing such a stunt. At the same time, I did not disbelieve her for a moment. To know Rosy was to know the truth when she spoke it. She was not always right, but she was always positive and equally truthful.

I could just picture her swinging that five-foot snake around, tottering from side to side, letting go to stumble in the direction of the projection, then struggling to regain her balance in the process.

Rosy is Happy Town's only permanent resident. She lives on the brink of poverty with no appearance of despair. She wouldn't have it any other way. She is resourceful enough to be there without resignation. She simply and completely accepts her place and her circumstances and is undaunted by a combination of infirmities that includes heart disease, diabetes, high blood pressure, arthritis, and diverticulitis, to say nothing of a recent cataract surgery.

Rosy does not drive. She is dependent on the good will of a few friends who help her out with occasional trips to the grocery store, the doctor's office, and her church. Visitors are infrequent. They include the rural mail carrier, the drug store delivery person, and myself.

Alive and Well

Rosy is one of a great and growing number of old folks on our contemporary social scene who live out their lives, most of the time, alone and all but forgotten. Others are closeted in the back rooms of relatives' homes, lost in nursing homes, or destitute on streets throughout the country.

At the same time, despite the muck and mire of governmental apathy, social services, dis-organizations, and the like, I am impressed with the multitude of services that are available to these bodies and souls.

Local community emergency medical services are prompt and dependable in aiding the Rosys of our area in times of urgent need. The 911 emergency service has been a savior for a lot of lives and has alleviated much suffering.

On my first visit, I could not have missed Happy Town, but I could have easily missed Rosy's place. I had to slow down my Chunker in order to spot it between a pair of large spruce trees. About a hundred feet off the berm of Butternut Road, her home looked like it had grown there over the years right along with trees and bushes. It took a discerning eye to distinguish the horizontal lines of the roof, porch, and windows from the surrounding vertical lines of nature's wild growth. I would have done better with a horse and buggy.

The Country Doctor

The only thing of modern vintage at Rosy's place was the mailbox placed on the corner of the porch. In bold letters, it announced the owner's resident, "Rosy Evans, Happy Town, U.S.A." In season, a woodchuck often stood by the post seemingly waiting for me, but it was quick to scurry under the porch floor as I approached.

Often, on the sunny June days of my visits, I would not leave Happy Town without stopping at the bank of the creek to sit, look, and listen for awhile.

"Crooked Creek," I would say aloud, for my own ears to hear, "how clean and clear you are, sparkling like an unending ribbon of diamonds bubbling through the soft green grasses of the bottom land.

"From the bosom of Mother Earth's mountains, you are the purest of nourishment for life within yourself and along your way.

"You are good medicine for me, too, and a big part of the reason why I live and practice among these hills and valleys."

I would not have been surprised had a mischievous Leprechaun peeked out from behind the mountain laurel.

I feel a quiet joy when I visit Rosy's place. To walk into her own little home is to go slowly and carefully through a cluttered kitchen into the crowded corner of her living room. She spends most of her day within a few square yards of a gas heater, a chair, and a small round

Alive and Well

table piled high with books and knitting. The remainder is spent on a pretty narrow path between the kitchen, bathroom, and bedroom (for her twice-daily naps).

I suppose most people would call Rosy's place dark and dingy. I could, too, if I allowed myself to pay close attention to the clutter. Withholding judgment, it's a step into the past of at least fifty years ago, something out of time and place, old and antiquish. I know Rosy feels it to be a cozy place, and I have to agree with her. She is more content with her circumstances in Happy Town, U.S.A. than she would be anywhere else in the world.

About every two weeks, Rosy calls the office just to have someone with whom she can chat for a few minutes. She complains of some dizziness now and then and hip pain that is left over from a fall she had two or three years ago. Her calls usually come on a Tuesday. It is her not so subtle way of making sure I will be visiting with her the following day.

Until I am inside Rosy's cottage, I am a bit on edge as I cross her field-like lawn and repeatedly yell my name to identify myself. My first visit, years ago, had prompted a double-barreled shotgun to slowly inch its way out the window to aim more or less in my direction. I kept yelling louder and louder, wondering about the intent at the other end of those barrels.

The Country Doctor

"Rosy, it's Dr. John! Remember?!" I held my black bag high over my head in surrender and sighed in grateful relief as the gun barrels withdrew from the open window and Rosy's face appeared.

Some of Rosy's acquaintances have told me that she acts strange at times, that she doesn't eat well, that she doesn't take very good care of herself.

"She's eccentric," they sometimes say. "She's not fit to live alone. She should be in a nursing home."

But, I know that Rosy is not strange. She's just smart. She plays the game of poor memory, managing to forget her purse when someone takes her to town for groceries and a stop at the restaurant. It is her way of getting a free meal.

Neither Rosy nor I ever agree with her friends' unsolicited opinions. To me, she has always been keen in her thinking and in her conversation. She makes much sense about herself, the weather, and time of day. I've come to see her as more physically and mentally right than those who try to tell me otherwise. The complainers are the ones who are not "right." Rosy is right, and so am I.

At the same time, I am concerned about the safety of her house. It was tumbling down at the time of my very first visit ten years ago. Boards were hanging loose here and there, the outer corner of the porch was sagging to

Alive and Well

the ground, bricks were missing from the chimney, and some of the window panes had cracked. Every time I look at it, I am careful not to look too directly or too hard, for fear of causing it to fall under the weight of my gaze. I do suspect that her "ivy-covered cottage," enshrouded with saplings and shrubs and wayward grapevines, might collapse some day in mortal demise. But, I would not be a part of forcing Rosy out of it for anything.

My other concern is Rosy's lack of compliance with the medicines I prescribe. Pill bottles are a constant, dazzling collage on her dining room table, along with a menagerie of things such as Kleenex®, toothpicks, pens, pencils, and other assorted items. Some of the pill bottles remain tightly capped, meaning that Rosy either does not or cannot open them. Others are opened and toppled over. Pills are scattered across the table and floor. Her unawareness of what they are and why they were prescribed is equal to her lack of recollection of when, and if, she took one or another. Having reached the age of ninety without them, Rosy gives them little regard. And I understand.

My monthly visit with Rosy is never complete until she again shows me her life's greatest treasure. Slowly, she trudges to her bedroom and takes a muskrat fur neckpiece out of a drawer.

The Country Doctor

"It was a special wedding gift from my husband sixty-five years ago," she tells me.

I express my surprise at its good condition. In the semi-darkness of her bedroom, I can't be sure that it isn't in good condition, and it certainly doesn't matter. I'm satisfied that it's not alive and moving just a wee little bit. I'm less sure it isn't alive with some little creatures who moved into the pelt over the years since the original owner was evicted.

On a very old, unused piano nearby, there is a faded wedding picture of Rosy and her husband.

"Did he live in this cottage with you?" I once asked.

"Yes he did, but not for long," she sadly replied.

She couldn't remember the length of time, but I knew she had lived alone for well over fifty years. They had no children of their own, and Rosy had outlived all known relatives.

Each time I visit Rosy's little place in the woods, I reflect on the many old folks I have known over the years in similar circumstances. Living quiet lives of isolation, doing little or nothing but sleeping, sitting, napping, eating, watching television, sometimes reading, knitting, and the like, is all they are physically and mentally able to do. It is definitely all that some of them are willing to do.

My wonder reflects further on what moves and motivates, what drives and allows these people to live on

Alive and Well

and on and on, even in the presence of multiple physical illnesses. I question what fundamental something keeps their vital functions going in the face of so much physical adversity. After forty years of thinking and feeling and wondering, I'm still surprised by it all.

As I drive away from Happy Town each time, with its sign in my rear view mirror, I am convinced that therein lies the answer. It is the smile on that sign and on Rosy's face and mine as we banter back and forth in friendly fun. She is as much a treat to me as I am to her.

Our parting comments end always with, "See ya in a few weeks, Rosy. Keep in touch and take care of yourself."

"Well, don't worry, I will. If I don't, no one else will."

And, she says that with such a sweet smile on her face and conviction in her voice.

Town sign near a small village: Slow--no hospital.

Interlude 38

Common Sense and Wellness
Some Highlights

1. Wellness is more than just not being sick.
2. It is looking, feeling, and being better.
3. It is something you can do for yourself.
4. It involves your total person: body, mind, and spirit.
5. It means common sense attention to:
   a. Your body:
      1) weight
      2) nutrition
      3) fitness
      4) bad habits - drugs, alcohol, tobacco, medication, overwork
      5) relaxation
   b. Your mind - stress without distress - mental relaxation
   c. Your spirit - relaxation for the soul
6. We are made up of equal physical, mental, and spiritual parts.

Alive and Well

7. Awareness - Acceptance - Allowance.
   a. Be Aware
      Of how you feel, think, behave.
   b. Be Accepting
      Of what you can't control with your heredity, environment, sex, age, weather.
      Of what you can control with diet, exercise, rest, stress, bad habits, attitude.
   c. Be Allowing
      Of a homeostases within yourself.
      Of an equilibrium with your environment and people.
      Of a balance with your physical, mental, and spiritual dimensions.

Chapter 39

There's No Place Like Home

*Home--Total and complete acceptance
of myself in my deepest heart.*

There is a virginal freshness to these tree-covered hills and valleys in the early morning, especially after a midsummer shower. The rain cleanses mountain country earth of dust and debris that have been accumulating during the hot and humid days of July. The air becomes crystal clear, and the tree canopy turns a bright, pulsing green.

Silver white wisps of misty fragments, leftover from the hemline of the passing rain, cling to the tenderloins of the slopes and suckle at the breast of the ridges. They dance through the air between each pair of hills and hover over the streams that flow dreamingly through the intricacies of the sensuous valleys.

Shimmering waters illuminate the scene with the bright sparkle of a diamond necklace clinging to the soft curves of the Mountain Princess. Background music becomes a symphony of wind and brook and stream as they flow ever onward in fulfillment of their mission to

Alive and Well

nurture plant and animal life along their journey to the seas. It is the playground of fairies and pixies and elves, of songbirds and butterflies, each playing their part in the composition of this special scene.

The first visit on my weekly house-call circuit is definitely my perpetual favorite. A brief pause at the fishing hole near the bridge where I once water-danced with fishes is always stop number one. These days, I am careful not to fall in as I fill the two-and-one-half-gallon jugs that Barbie uses to water her subtropical array of house plants. The plants fill most of the sun room from floor to ceiling, growing with lush exuberance under her nurturing hands.

Her fingers are as green as her thumbs. It seems that the hearts of Barbie and the plants are equally full of love for each other, and they both appreciate that clear, pure, mountain stream water.

A special bond is evident when Barbie and plants and wildflowers are in each other's presence. I can sense them communicating as she hums and speaks to them in a soft, musical voice, and they respond in barely audible, purring sound. I imagine their little leaves and petals and branches reaching out to squeeze her fingers and to touch her ever so gently with a sweet, subliminal feeling that permeates the air.

The Country Doctor

Water, you know, is a spiritual medium, most especially when mountain pure. It speaks to all of earth's inhabitants, be they animal, plant, or mineral. A favorite pause in Barbie's busy day includes quiet time on the bank of a stream. As the trickling flow sings a song of serenity to her, the water's surface sparkles like an endless string of diamonds in its journey to return to the clouds that gave it birth, and Barbie returns to herself.

Although called a plateau, mountain country is by no means flat. Innumerable, seemingly endless, ridges are densely covered with deciduous trees. Valleys are narrow, and the bottomlands are small and few. The flat tops of most of them are often less than a few dozen acres.

The summit and the slopes of the hills are wrinkled by numerous grooves that appear to have been scratched by monstrous prehistoric claws. The markings etch down the slopes into increasingly larger ravines, then into valleys that exit the foothills into the bottomland. Uncounted seeps and springs give birth to virgin-pure waters that expand into small brooks which stop temporarily in various-sized lakes, then flow onward as mighty rivers that disappear in coastal seas.

The Allegheny plateau is unique in its contribution of its headwaters to watersheds on each side of the eastern continental divide that end in the Chesapeake Bay eastward and the Gulf of Mexico southward.

Alive and Well

An outer-space view of Allegheny mountain country shows the high plateaus, ridges, and valleys as breakers at an ocean shore. Southward and eastward, the summits become gradually lower and further apart with increasingly wider bottomlands in between. Broad expanses of farmland emerge at the southern extent, as though the northern breakers have calmed themselves into the rolling swells of the sea.

To experience the inner spaces of the valleys and bottomlands, convinces me that I am in the heart of the world and the soul of the universe. The cozy intimacy of the deep narrow valleys is a constant re-creation of post-conception, prebirth, and womb room comfort. The spirituality of living in the land is comparable to never having left that blissful former life. And for me, to live this wonderful mountain country scene is definitely a special circumstance of birth.

To dwell, to labor and frolic between the outer and inner spaces of Allegheny mountain brigadoons is to share Garden of Eden plant and animal life with Appalachian Mountain inhabitants all the way from Maine to Georgia.

I remember a day that my house call brought me into the cleft of two deep ridges in the direction of the highest summit in these parts. Out of my daze-dreaming along the way, I could see a figure between the road and

The Country Doctor

the stream ahead of me. He was jumping around in a wild pantomime and holding one hand over his mouth. The other grasped a fishing pole.

We recognized each other at the same time. As I approached, he was alternately holding his hand to his mouth and waving it frantically in my direction.

"Barney!" I yelled. "I know you're glad to see me, but you've never greeted me with such enthusiasm before. What in the world is the matter?"

He was trying to talk in a strange muffled shriek, unable to move his lips.

"Take your hand away so I can have a look," I instructed.

He did so with a mixture of reluctance and embarrassment. The fishing hook at the end of his line had pierced through his lower lip, then buried itself halfway through his upper.

"Well, Barney, I'm not going to ask you how you did that. I may not ever let you forget it either."

Taking the pole into my hand, I led him to the grassy bank of the nearby stream.

"Lay down here and be still. We're going to take that hook out right now. There is no way you can get to the office. I am going to numb your lips with cold-water compresses so that you won't feel the novocaine injection. Hold absolutely still."

Alive and Well

I administered one injection into his lower lip along the shoulder of the hook, the other into the upper lip at the tip of the barb.

"Now, keep the cold compresses over your mouth while I get a pair of wire cutters from the truck."

After I pushed the end of the hook through his upper lip and cut it off just below the barb, I slipped the rest of the hook back through his lower lip at its point of entry.

"There, it's done. How does it feel?" I asked.

"My lips feel fat," Barney uttered, "but I don't hurt. They're just numb."

"You'll be all right now. Just take it easy for the rest of the day. Relax and keep cold compresses over your mouth. I'll see you in the office tomorrow to give you a tetanus booster and check for infection."

Barney is an exception among the young people in small mountain towns like mine. The majority of them are quick to leave when they graduate high school. College or other career opportunities draw them away. Most of them never return except for holiday and vacation visits.

As a result, some rural communities do not grow and develop. Many slowly fade into small villages and crossroads. Others stay about the same due to "downstate" folk who retire to small, tranquil country towns and to outdoorsmen attracted by hunting and

The Country Doctor

fishing opportunities during their working lives. As for Barney, I knew that he would never leave.

His roots are too deep. He has been captured by the mystery and magic of the natural world and all its fundamental wonders. I also knew that, with a few more years of maturity, he would learn to keep himself off both ends of a fishing line at the same time.

As Barney headed home, I drove deeper into the valley and climbed steadily upward. Five minutes and two miles later, I was on top of the world. At 2,500 feet above sea level and 800 feet above the stream in the valley, that summit is a place for seeing and a time for being. From there, I was able to see some forty miles over rolling hills and undulating valleys to infinity in the skies overhead, into the years of age inside myself.

Despite the magnitude of distance and the depth of time, there is a strong, living intimacy with all that is within the panoramic view. I daze-dream the image of my being over the lay of the land; valley over hill, hill in valley. It is as perfect and comfortable a match as a pair of lovers in close embrace. There is that kind of fit between me and this land and my place on it.

Each time I visit that special summit, a swarm of forgotten memories flutter across my mind, taunting my presence with fleeting and flippant butterfly fragments from out of my past. They are the seeds for here and now

Alive and Well

which will grow into the sweet recollections of a time now bred, but not yet born.

And so it is that the seasons of this good earth and those of my life walk hand in hand over these hills and through these valleys. We have shared the growing green of spring, the exuberant Roman-candle burst of summer wildflowers, the flaming foliage of autumn, and the quiet, white snows of resting winter. In meditative moments, I flip the pages of its days from one point to another and around again to where I began.

I can feel an intimacy with all God's precious creations, the celestial, the terrestrial, the animal, vegetable, and mineral. I feel the depth of that closeness with an intensity equal to that of the roots that bred and bore and nurtured me deep in the spring of my youth.

In my own ongoing moments of reflective appreciation, I, like most of us, contemplate life after life and wonder what it will be for me. It would be enough if it were the equal to my here and now. I wish for no outer-space celestial city with streets of gold, only the wonder that is already with me, bonded by the magic and the mystery of natural wonders.

Having reached four-score years of age less six and being as healthy as I was at half this age, I am well on my way for leaving, but not yet gone. When I go, I hope to

The Country Doctor

transcend to this heaven on earth followed by no more than a brief thought and a quiet whisper.

Meanwhile, back at the office, the walls are decorated with a collage of three pieces of fish hook and line, a broken arrow that missed its mark, a skinning knife from a hapless hunter who severed a finger while dressing a deer, tongue depressors complete with name, date, and number of black-silk sutures removed from dozens of children treated for lacerations, and photographs of wide-smiled young hunters and fishermen showing their prize turkey, deer, bear, or fish!

Something's wrong, Doctor.
I've never felt this well before.

Interlude 39

Patient Wisdom

After forty years of medical practice, I am pretty well convinced that much of what I know has come from my patients, even if it has been a process of re-learning rather than learning for the first time.

One day, my lesson came from a country gentleman in all-around good health who gave me his prescription for proper eating for weight maintenance. His way was to have his largest meal of the day for breakfast, a moderate-sized lunch, and a light supper. Now what could be any more sensible than that? His method could serve as an answer to those people who say, "It's not what I eat that causes my obesity. It's the way I eat that does me in."

The truth of the matter is that what and how much you eat do count, not when or in what way you consume it. If you eat more calories than you burn, the extras become excess weight.

Mr. H. had some other good ideas that worked well for him. His diet included liberal amounts of fish and fowl as well as fiber, fruits, and vegetables. He made an important point of refraining from sauces and dressings,

The Country Doctor

the culprits that can sometimes add more calories to a meal than the food itself.

That same patient also reminded me of the importance of exercise. Mr. H. knew from his own experience that diet is only half of what it takes. The other half is exercise, some form of exercise for a half hour to an hour at least four to five days a week. He went fly fishing in the summer and honed his wood-crafting skills the rest of the year, along with a daily dose of walking three to five miles at a steady pace until he worked up a pant and a sweat.

Mr. H. always had a quick gem of medical wisdom to leave with me at the end of each visit. On one particular day, he told me about a sudden, sharp lightning-like pain he had experienced on the top of his foot several days previous. He put direct finger pressure on the spot, held it firmly for about a minute, and had instant and lasting relief. It was a nonspecific neuritis-type pain, and that's what acupressure can do for you.

Chapter 40

A Long, Long Trail A-Winding

A legend is a truth on its way to becoming a myth.

A trail, now, is a pathway for walking from one place to another.

It is usually found meandering through fields and forests and over country roads in the great outdoors. Unlike walkways in towns and shopping malls, a trail covers distances of hundreds of feet to many hundreds of miles.

Hiking trails exist throughout the country and are used by tens of thousands of people each year in summer and winter, in rain or shine. In addition to fun and fitness, experiencing the manifold pleasures of nature can result in aches and pains, sprains and strains, bumps and bruises, bites and stings, and blisters.

So, too, it can be responsible for an occasional stroke or heart attack, broken bones, and other major catastrophes.

Therefore, there is a time and a place for country doctoring on the trail. Most often it consists of rendering first aid and paying careful attention to prevention and

The Country Doctor

common sense. Rarely is it necessary to summon a life-flight helicopter!

The North Country National Scenic Trail is one of a network of trails encompassing and crisscrossing the United States from the north country to the south and from sea to shining sea. It is the longest one, an estimated 4,200 miles.

The eastern trail head, in the upper northeastern corner of New York, leads southwestward on to 625 miles of trail that exit the Empire State at Allegheny State Park and enter the Keystone State near Kinzua Dam. It then crosses the northwestern corner of Pennsylvania for a distance of 300 miles to enter the southeastern corner of Ohio.

The Buckeye State boasts a distance of 1,050 miles of trail which encircles the entire state to enter southcentral Michigan and continue northward then westward for another 1,150 miles. After a long and winding path north to the Upper Peninsula, it takes a fairly straight shot across MacKinac Island, to cross through Wisconsin for a distance of 220 miles. It then takes on an upside down, boot shaped trek through Minnesota to arrive at Lake Sakakawea, near the center of North Dakota. There, after it has crossed the

Alive and Well

headwaters of the Mississippi River, it ends to connect with the Lewis and Clark Trail.

Should a long, long distance hiker complete the trail (probably a year or so after starting out), he or she would have traveled through all four seasons of the temperate north country and taken more steps than the average pedometer could handle. If one stride is assumed to be about three feet, the number of steps per mile would amount to 1,760. When multiplied by 4,200 miles, a very conservative estimate of the number of steps required to travel the entire trail is 7,392,000. I suspect the number would be closer to 10,000,000 if one considers the many short strides over and around rocks and streams and a multitude of other obstacles.

A special feature of the North Country Trail, compared to other historic and scenic trails, is that it is more latitudinal than longitudinal. The east to west rather than the north to south direction allows for a great diversity of terrain, scenery, geology, and plant life. Its warp in time parallels the early history of the American westward movement.

Another of the trail's greatest assets is a host of volunteers, comprising the membership of the North Country Trail Association. While most historic and scenic trails are supported by governments and contributing organizations, this trail's birth, growth, and development

The Country Doctor

owes its existence to an eager and enthusiastic legion of dedicated members.

The country's system of national, historic, and scenic trails was implemented in 1968 when it was signed into law by President Johnson after much pioneering by visionary individuals as far back as the early 1900's. The trails are non-motorized. Motorcycles, snowmobiles, and other engine-driven vehicles are forbidden.

It is this remarkable and extensive system of trails which give myriads of Americans access to unlimited natural beauty, wildlife, native plants and wildflowers, and the opportunity for physical, mental, and spiritual interconnection and balance within themselves and with others.

At the same time, despite the likeliest of expectations and the best-formed plans of hikers, bikers, skiers, snowshoers, runners, and horses, the strange and the bizarre can happen.

One such occurrence had its beginning some twenty-five hundred years ago in the northern part of the British Isles. A great many Irish people, men and women alike, became so crowded in old England they no longer had room to play with their shillelaghs. They could no longer tolerate the English either, and decided to leave the country and sail westward to find a new land.

Alive and Well

They had an uneventful journey until they approached the coast of what is now known as New England. Within several miles of shore, the wildest of storms came upon them. It was later named Typhoon Brogue, and it generated a tidal wave so powerful that it swept their ship onto the beach where it came to rest on a mountain of red lobsters (a place now called Katahdin).

The woeful Irish men and women who stared down over the slope at that huge mound of crustaceans claimed that it smelled pretty fishy. The travelers were so green with fright that future generations became known as leprechauns.

The lobsters were not very pleased with the predicament either. They became red in the face with anger and, with their vicious, snapping pinchers, they attacked the intruders.

For the Irish, farther west was the only safe way to go. They streaked rapidly westward in a somewhat helter-skelter manner over a corridor of about twenty miles wide, for a distance of some four thousand miles, until they came to rest at a neat lake in the midst of a great, grassy plain. It just so happened that the route they established paved the groundwork of what was later adopted as today's North Country Trail.

The Country Doctor

The Irish people left New England so fast that all they had time to salvage were their shillelaghs, blarney stones, and blueberry seedlings. Those three items contributed greatly to their survival. They used their shillelaghs to obtain small animals and upland game birds for food. The blarney stones became trail markers to blaze the trail for future hikers and other non-motorized travelers. Blueberry seedlings were planted in the bottomland of valleys along the way, and they grew there with unbounded abandon, wide and deep, over the years. They produced a tasty fruit for baked goods and jams and juice for fermenting a special drink for wintertime. The bushes became dense and strong enough to walk on, to ride horseback, to support dwellings, and accommodate all other requirements for everyday living.

Twenty-five hundred years later, a pair of hikers were backpacking the North Country Trail near the outer edge of one of those blueberry bogs. They came to a neat looking place where they chose to camp for the night and have blueberries for a bedtime snack.

After taking a skinny dip in the pristine waters of nearby Lake Lubber, they browsed around for the best and biggest berries of all. It was then that they noticed a spot where the bushes were compressed into a saucer shape some two yards wide and eight feet long. The

Alive and Well

outline began to take on a familiar shape. The couple's wide, blue eyes looked closer to discover some strands of shining black hairs, which no doubt belonged to a very large bear who had spent the night on the comfort of the blueberry bog mattress.

They became alarmed that the monstrous creature might still be in the immediate vicinity. They no more than voiced their concerns to each other than they heard a thunderous roar. A mountain of a black bear came running toward them with wide open jaws. In its throat was a pair of tonsils the size of bowling balls. Not having asked the bear to, "say ahh," they figured he was up to no good for the two of them.

What to do? No weapons! No time to run! The inevitable happened. John quickly disappeared into that wide open mouth.

Barbie had the quick sense to grab him by his ankles just as he was about to disappear from sight. She planted her heels into the bushes and pulled as hard as she could until John snapped out of the bear's interior!

In the meantime, he grabbed the bear by the root of his tail and pulled him inside out with his own exit. The bear was so embarrassed by this sudden turn of his own event, that he whirled around to get away as quickly as possible, wondering which way to go. And that's the bear truth now.

The Country Doctor

John felt like Jonah after he had escaped from the belly of the whale and returned home to stand at the doorway, soaking wet, dripping with seaweed dangling from his shoulders.

His wife had exclaimed, "Jonah! Where have you been? You smell like a fish."

After John had his own feet planted firmly on the ground, and the bear was high-tailing it inside out toward the woods, Barbie asked, "John, how do you feel? You look a bit wooky."

"I feel like a worn-out stock market--very bearish."

By this time you will realize that this country doctor's times on the trail often have very little to do with doctoring. Hours spent are ninety-nine percent or more recreational, diversionary, fun, and fancy. So, too, has been the sharing of myself and my patients with you.

As the journey over the trail and through these pages comes to a close, I end on a more whimsical note with the hope that this long, long trail a-winding will connect us with each other again somewhere along the way, on the trail and in the second volume of *The Country Doctor . . . Alive and Well.*

Footnote: The credibility of this story can be confirmed by a search of the North Country Trail

Alive and Well

headquarters archives in the section, True Tall Tales of the North Country Trail under the title *A Tail of One Big Bear and Two Little Bares.* The subtitle is, *The Bear Came Over the Mountain to See What He Could See, and the Only Thing He Saw Was Another Side of Himself.*

*I looked in the mirror one day and
discovered my identity--me.*

About the Author

Dr. John has been a medical doctor for forty years after preparing himself with three years as a World War II U.S. Navy Corpsman, an Allegheny College biology and chemistry major, a University of Pennsylvania medical student, a Wilmington, Delaware Hospital intern, and a University of Pittsburgh Medical Center resident in occupational and environmental medicine.

The doctor has taken his commonsense and compassionate approach to medicine, coupled with the spirit of the country doctor, from the rural Allegheny Mountains to the Dakota and Montana Indian country, the African countries of Ethiopia and Sudan, Pennsylvania Correctional Institutions, and back again to Rainbow's End Nature Sanctuary in Cameron County, Pennsylvania. He provides consulting services for occupational, environmental, alternative, and holistic medicine as personal physician to individuals and families, family doctor to the workplace (employee and employer), and as country doctor to the environment.

The doctor and his wife live, work, and love there, offering sanctuary to indigenous wild plant and animal life and to patients, friends, and acquaintances. Rainbow's End is a multidimensional center for promoting the physical, psychological, and spiritual well being of humankind, the earth, and the universe.

Personal Health Services include:

- Comprehensive General Health Assessment
- Chronic Fatigue
- Chronic Pain
- Fibromyalgia
- Chemical Toxicity and Sensitivity
- Weight Management
- Personal Injury Evaluation
- Worker's Compensation Evaluation
- Counseling for Whole Health

Future plans include onsite workshops and seminars on a wide variety of subjects; i.e., landscape design with native shrubs and wildflowers, healthy homes and buildings, nature photography and writing, environmental aesthetics, the magic of the daytime sky, and the mystery of the sky at night.

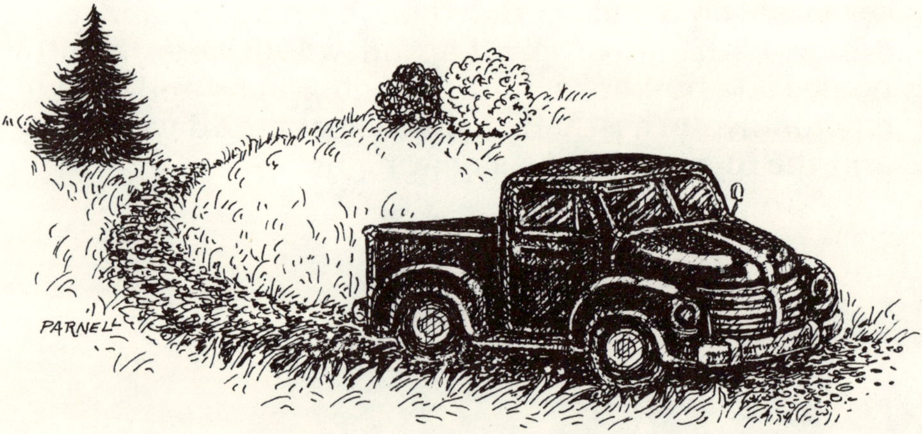
PARNELL

To order additional copies . . .

. . . of *The Country Doctor, Alive and Well*, complete the information below.

Name:	No. of Books @ $19.95 per book		$_____
Address:	PA Residents add 6% Sales Tax To Book Price Only		$_____
City:	Shipping and Handling - US Mail		$_____
State: Postal Code:			
	Orders up to	$20.00	$4.95
Daytime Phone:	$20.01 to	$40.00	$5.95
	$40.01 to	$60.00	$7.95
Call for shipping and handling	$60.01 to	$80.00	$10.95
on orders over $100.00 (US),	$80.01 to	$100.00	$12.95
Overseas, UPS, or 2-Day Air.	Total		$_____

Payment Method: ____Check   ____Money Order   ____Visa   ____MasterCard

Card#_____ Expiration_____

Authorized Signature_____

Allow 4-6 weeks for delivery

Mail entire page with payment to:
Good Earth Publishing
RR 1 North Creek
P.O. Box 243
Emporium, PA 15834
Phone: (814) 486-2084
Fax: (814) 486-2438
www.thecountrydoctor.com

A Caring Concern for the Environment; Humankind, Earth, Universe

The Country Doctor, Alive and Well is available at quantity discount. For more information, call (888) 725-9495 or fax (814) 486-2438. You will find *The Country Doctor, Alive and Well* a wonderful gift for family, friends, associates, a friendly traveling companion, and a special addition to your own self help bookshelf. Book available from the publisher at the above address or from book stores, gift shops, and other fine stores nationwide. Help get the Country Doctor message out to all parts of our country and to all countries of the world, to people as patients and patients as people who need, and want and wish.

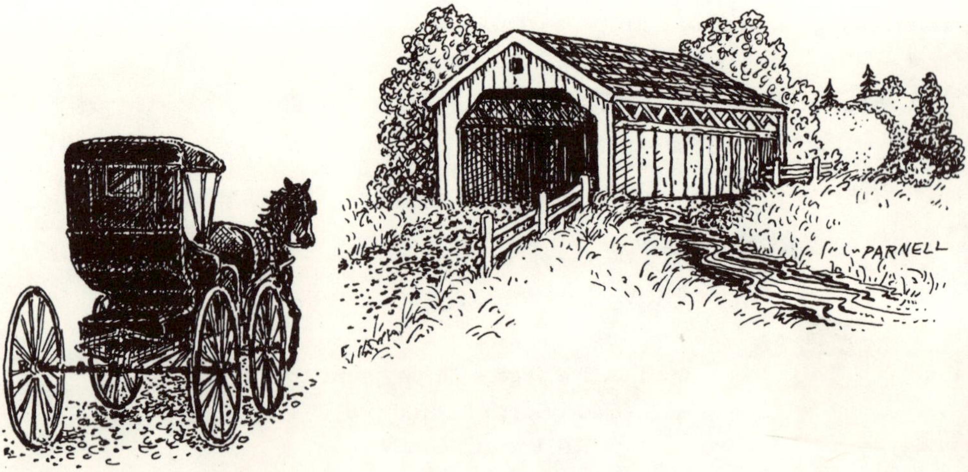
PARNELL